dbmiller@ambs.edu

5.40

STORMFRONT

THE BOOKSTORE

THE GOSPEL AND OUR CULTURE SERIES

A series to foster the missional encounter of the gospel
with North American culture

Lois Y. Barrett

General Editor

• •

Volumes now available

James V. Brownson, Inagrace T. Dietterich, Barry A. Harvey,
and Charles C. West, *StormFront: The Good News of God*

Darrell L. Guder, *The Continuing Conversion of the Church*

Darrell L. Guder, ed., *Missional Church: A Vision for the
Sending of the Church in North America*

George R. Hunsberger, *Bearing the Witness of the Spirit:
Lesslie Newbigin's Theology of Cultural Plurality*

Craig Van Gelder, editor, *Confident Witness — Changing World:
Rediscovering the Gospel in North America*

Forthcoming

Lois Y. Barrett et al., *Treasure in Clay Jars:
Patterns in Missional Faithfulness*

STORMFRONT

The Good News of God

James V. Brownson
Inagrace T. Dietterich
Barry A. Harvey
Charles C. West

with a Foreword by

George R. Hunsberger

WILLIAM B. EERDMANS PUBLISHING COMPANY
GRAND RAPIDS, MICHIGAN / CAMBRIDGE, U.K.

© 2003 Wm. B. Eerdmans Publishing Co.
All rights reserved

Wm. B. Eerdmans Publishing Co.
255 Jefferson Ave. S.E., Grand Rapids, Michigan 49503 /
P.O. Box 163, Cambridge CB3 9PU U.K.

Printed in the United States of America

10 09 08 07 06 05   8 7 6 5 4 3 2

ISBN-10: 0-8028-2225-8 / ISBN-13: 978-0-8028-2225-3

www.eerdmans.com

Contents

FOREWORD

The Story That Chooses Us

Galadriel: The world is changed. I feel it in the water. I feel it in the earth. I smell it in the air. Much that once was, is lost, for none now live who remember it.

J. R. R. TOLKIEN, *The Fellowship of the Rings*

The world changes. There are times when we know that. Once familiar storylines take a sharp turn this way or that or vanish altogether. Fragments of memory grow pale. Patchwork imaginings stir only the faintest of hopes that some story may again find the world and nourish it back to life.

But which story? And which telling of it? Maybe it has been more true of other times than we have thought, but in our time, at least, the contending parables multiply. No longer does a single story hold it all together. Each of us is under a funny kind of obligation to find our own, make up our own, claim our own.

All the while, Christian storytellers live in the grip of an ancient-present story centered in the life, death, and resurrection of Jesus. They have found that this story has read them inside and out, it has laid bare their motives and the movements of their spirits. It has captured them into its still unfolding drama. They know the experience of Frodo — the Hobbit hero of J. R. R. Tolkien's classic, now cinematized, trilogy —

who without willing it or wanting it came into possession of a ring whose own adventure changed everything in the path of his life. Not only had the ring chosen Frodo. The responsibility to see the ring to the fires of Mordor for its destruction had chosen him as well. And the company who shared "this sort of . . . mission . . . quest . . . thing" (to quote Frodo's companion, Pippin) was implicated in the choosing.

The job of telling "gospel" — the good news of God — is always a fresh challenge that requires the teller to have ears to hear and eyes to see. Many of the older ways the story has been told are ready at hand, ways shaped by other times and places that demanded certain tones and accents if the story was to be heard in a way that was true to its first telling. But as the Christian story gets told over and over in a given place, it can as easily as not be overpowered by other claims and visions that absorb it into their own agendas. So it has been in the North American scene. Gradually, many of us have been driven back to our origins with ears and eyes eager to see, to hear, to know that first story. And we are stirred to render it fresh for this new time and place.

The four authors of this book testify that the good news of God has captured them. Whether or not they ever thought otherwise, they know now that the significant thing is not that they chose to hold to the story for some personal benefit, real or imagined. Rather, they know the story came as the news of God that required the allegiance of their lives. It has worked its ever-more compelling power on them to put them to this way, this quest, this mission. It is this that makes them — and the rest of us who are thus captured — the church.

Several years ago, the authors took up a challenge presented to them by companions in the Gospel and Our Culture Network. They set out to achieve what they have come to call "a faithful and compelling performance of the gospel." They wanted to say as clearly and directly as possible what they hear to be the good news of God, as told in the Christian Scriptures and as it bears on the peculiar ways of life of today's North Americans.

The word "performance" has a very particular meaning when used this way. It is not used in the sense of entertainment. Rather, it is used in reference to the way any language functions. A performance of a language is not the language itself, with all its established conventions of grammar, fields of meaning, etc. It is an act of speech uttered by someone in that language. Such an utterance corresponds to the conventions of the language enough to be understood by others who know the language, and thus it communicates meaning. But it is an utterance distinct to the user at a particular moment, an example of the use of the language.

Let me illustrate from the days when my children were learning to understand and speak English. My daughter Lauren, when she was very young, stirred us to laughter one day with one of her attempts to speak our common language. She had obviously observed adult speech "performances" and had detected from them the way English works. Hearing others express in one way or another something like, "That's a good idea," and learning which moments might bring forth such an expression, she decided to try it out for herself. The right moment arrived, and she made the attempt: "That could be a idea!" Her performance of the language was a true and fitting use of it, while just odd enough in the particulars to bring us a good laugh. We still chuckle decades later when we remember that early performance. (She hasn't stopped talking since, and her performances of the English language have come to have an incisive and polished quality. Not to mention the sheer number of them!)

This book is a performance of the gospel of God. The first record we have of that gospel, of course, are the earliest documents of the Christian tradition. Those documents of the New Testament have a privileged place for setting the grammar, establishing the language of the story, and thereby setting in place the kinds of understanding appropriate to it. The reiteration of the news in this book is a performance tested by its correspondence to those Scriptures. It is also to be tested by how well it hears and reads their nuances in a way that connects with the deep reverberations of the human spirit in the soul of today's North America.

The written, verbal performance of good news presented here is offered in clear recognition that the daily lived performance by vibrant communities of Christ is the most fundamental testament to the gospel's force and power. The lived performance is the more compelling and crucial. It is that which will tell what is live-able about this ancient-present story. In one sense, this book simply attempts to give articulation to what is important in those lived performances that are all around us.

On the other hand, this book has something important to say to those Christian communities. It encourages them to give greater attention to their responsibility to give the good news of God its lived expression. The authors offer them a fresh and challenging vision, gleaned from the Scriptures and played against the backdrop of the way our culture has tended to tame and distort the gospel. They argue for the renewing capacity of a fresh, sensitive hearing of the gospel and offer it to encourage the church to make faithfulness to the gospel its greatest aim.

When the authors tell us here what the good news of God is, it is obvious that to them this is a "story that chooses us," much as Frodo found himself to be chosen. The threads of the storyline are woven in this direction.

We live in an ever-swirling *storm.*

> *Gandalf [to a despairing Frodo]:* There is more at work in this world than the force of Evil. Bilbo was meant to have the Ring, in which case you also were meant to have it. And that is an encouraging thought.

The coming reign of God, now entered into our affairs in the person of Jesus, sets in motion the collision of systems of rule and authority. It is along such a storm front as this that the church finds itself called into being and implicated on the side of what God is still steadily and faithfully intending for the world, a world in which there is "more at work than the force of evil." And that is an encouraging thought.

We live in a contest of *allegiance.*

> *Frodo:* I wish the ring had never come to me. I wish none of this had happened.
>
> *Gandalf:* So do all who live to see such times. But that is not for them to decide. All we have to decide is what to do with the time that is given to us.

Decision. That is the critical matter put before everyone we meet in the Gospels when they come face to face with Jesus. Not a decision about what might be in one's rational self-interest. But a decision about what now must be done "with the time that is given to us."

We live in a life and death *communion.*

> *Aragorn:* The same blood flows in my veins. The same weakness.
> *Arwen:* Your time will come. You will face the same evil, and you
> will defeat it.

The ordinary path of life for Christ-followers is one of deep inner
rootedness in the life and death of Jesus. It is the good news of God
that we are welcomed into the dying and rising of Jesus, by which he
faced the evil and defeated even the final enemy, death. That sharing in
Christ is what carves out the shape of the calling, the mission, the
sending of the church.

We live at the intersection of *powers.*

> *Frodo [speaking about Gollum]:* It's a pity Bilbo didn't kill him when
> he had the chance.
> *Gandalf:* Pity? It was pity that stayed Bilbo's hand. Many that de-
> serve life receive death and many that deserve death do not re-
> ceive it. Can you give that to them?

Subtle or not so subtle, direct or indirect, overt or covered with layers of
pretense, the powers of our world represent profound patterns of resistance to the power of God, coming as it has in the form of a cross.
Cross-bearing resistance comes in the form of pity, not vengeance;
mercy, not violence; life-giving in place of death-dealing.

We live in a crucible of *practices.*

> *Galadriel:* The Quest stands upon the edge of a knife. Stray but a lit-
> tle, and it will fail, to the ruin of all. Yet hope remains while the
> Company is true.

Christian practices, churchly practices, are the implication of all this
for the life of the church. But not merely practices in the sense of orga-
nizational activities. Rather, radical, even subversive, practices are
called for, practices that Jesus anticipates in what have been called the
Beatitudes. "Stray but a little. . . . Hope remains while the Company is
true."

Is this a faithful performance of the gospel? I believe it is. Faithfulness is about hearing, feeling, knowing what was said at the outset that sets the path for what is rightly called Christian. It is always an exercise in community, wrestling to say the gospel with a common voice, as these four authors have done. It has been their experience that their own different takes on the gospel have pushed them each to keep that faith more fully — not captivated by a current trend, nor pretending that they can do anything other than give a reading, a rendering in this time and place, with the mental and language tools our culture gives us, of what was originally announced as the good news. This is no search for some "pure gospel unadulterated by any cultural accretions" — which, as Lesslie Newbigin has had to remind so many of us in the West, is in any case an illusion (see *Foolishness to the Greeks*, p. 4). Rather, it is a search for a careful and powerful way of putting this story for this generation.

Over several years' time, the authors became a community of discernment together. Their experience was such that at the end of their work they determined to own the message of the book together. So they are listed as co-authors of the whole, not as authors of individual essays. In the process of the writing, each chapter was first drafted by one of them, then wrestled over by the group. In each case, the contribution of the drafting hand remains in the final version, and the authors permit me here to identify which hand shaped each chapter. Barry Harvey, associate professor of theology at Baylor University, drafted the first chapter ("Storm") and offered the imagery that ultimately set the pace for the whole. Jim Brownson, academic dean and professor of New Testament at Western Theological Seminary, drafted the second and third chapters ("Allegiance" and "Communion"), drawing on the New Testament's ways of signaling what lies at the heart of the gospel. Charles West, emeritus professor of ethics at Princeton Theological Seminary, drafted the fourth chapter ("Powers") showing what is at stake as the gospel encounters the world's systems of life and imagination. Inagrace Dietterich, director of theological research at the Center for Parish Development, drafted the final chapter ("Practices") about the way of life to which the Christian community is chosen.

Surely the authors would want to join me in expressing gratitude to the broader community that nurtured this manuscript to its present form. Numerous members of the Gospel and Our Culture Network visited with them around the themes of their work at several of the network's annual consultations and reflected on some of their working papers published in *The Gospel and Our Culture* newsletter. Even more explicit help came from a group of twelve people who were invited to review an early form of the manuscript and spend a day with the authors to share their responses. The group included Darren Cummings, Ted Newell, Bob Lynn, Mary Motte fmm, Mark Lau Branson, Bill McConville OFM, Amy Castello, and Philip Kenneson. Arrangements for that meeting and all the meetings of the authors along the way in this multiyear project were handled by Judy Bos with the kind of personal care and hospitality that make the message of this book credible.

Toward the end of the process, Laurie Baron's editorial assistance proved to be invaluable as she worked through the manuscript to provide the consistency of language, style, and intent that would help Christian readers travel and celebrate the road the authors were laying out. For each of the authors, the personal support of their families, colleagues, and friends provided the encouragement necessary to complete the project. The financial resources for all of this work were provided by a grant from the Lilly Endowment, whose help with this and other efforts of The Gospel and Our Culture Network is deeply appreciated.

Finally, a concluding note or two. This telling of the gospel is for the Christian reader and his or her Christian community. It promises to prod the continuing conversion that the Spirit intends for the church and for all who are a part of it. In this respect, the book promises to be useful in a variety of ways: as a guide for small group discussion, for formative processes of *catechesis* into Christian faith, for renewals of the faith in Advent or Lenten seasons, and many more.

But this telling of the gospel is not only for Christians; it is for all. The book offers to tell what is most compelling about the good news of God for the kind of world we now are. It is a book that spiritual seekers may discuss profitably with those seasoned in the way of Christian discipleship in order to discover this story of God's intentions, and to be discovered by it. As it points to what is coming, by the grace of God, it shows the stuff of which hope is made.

GEORGE R. HUNSBERGER

1

STORM

God Addresses the Spirit of the Age

"If you don't like the way you were born — try being born again!" This announcement, prominently displayed recently on a church marquee in my neighborhood, reflects perfectly the spirit of religious life in North America today. It advertises to all who pass by the church what sounds like very good news: "If you don't like who you are now, God has a 'new you' ready to try on! Details available inside!"[1] This is exactly the kind of message that modern men and women like to hear. What could be better news than to hear that the God who called the universe into existence wants nothing more than to make us over into what we most want to be?

How could this message not be compelling? As a result of years of cultural conditioning, recent generations in North America have come to see themselves almost exclusively as consumers whose sole purpose in life is to satisfy their individual needs. Yet the four of us who wrote this book are convinced that the message displayed on that church marquee fails to reflect accurately or faithfully what the gospel is all about. Quite frankly, it is woefully inadequate to the hope that is ours in Christ Jesus. Not only does this message by itself leave much to be desired, it is also symptomatic of a widespread problem within the church today, which is to confuse the gospel with an infomercial, and

---

1. More recently, another church demonstrated its knowledge of good marketing: "Free Coffee, Eternal Life: Membership Has Its Privileges."

the community of God's people with vendors of spiritual goods and services.

We have set for ourselves a very difficult task in these pages, for we shall be inviting you to consider a vision of what the God revealed in Jesus Christ is up to in the world that is very different from the one displayed on the church marquee. We do not agree on every detail of this vision, and from time to time some of those disagreements will show up. At stake in the vision we follow is nothing less than the church's identity, its reason for existing at all. We believe that the church exists to participate in God's redemptive work in the world. This work takes as its focus not our wants and desires, but the way of life, the suffering and the triumph, of Jesus. The gospel is not just a message to be proclaimed; it is the form of our participation in what God is doing in and for the world.

Our way of describing this participation in God's redemptive work is to say that the good news of Jesus Christ is *missional* from beginning to end. Mission is not simply something the church does. Rather, as the authors of *Missional Church* put it, "it is the result of God's initiative, rooted in God's purposes to restore and heal creation. 'Mission' means 'sending' and it is the central biblical theme describing the purpose of God's action in human history."[2] God's mission begins within the life of the triune God, as the Father sends the Son in the incarnation and the Spirit to the church. This twofold sending unfolds in history in the call of the people of Israel to bear God's blessing to all the families of the earth. The story of God's people is narrated in Scripture and reaches its zenith in the work of Jesus for the salvation of the world. The Spirit is then poured out on the followers of Jesus to extend the work of redemption and reconciliation to every part of the earth. The mission of God "continues today in the worldwide witness of churches in every culture to the gospel of Jesus Christ, and it moves toward the promised consummation of God's salvation in the *eschaton* ('last' or 'final day')."[3] When considered from this standpoint of sending, the gospel has less to do with the alleged benefits that might come with believing in God and more with what God plans to do *with* those who answer Jesus' call to give up all and follow him.

---

2. Darrell L. Guder, ed., *Missional Church: A Vision for the Sending of the Church in North America* (Grand Rapids: Eerdmans, 1998), p. 4.

3. Guder, ed., *Missional Church*, p. 4.

A Consuming Culture

Someone once observed that we do not know who first discovered water, but we are fairly sure that it was not a fish. That is to say, it is relatively easy to recognize when something out of the ordinary comes along, but we tend not to notice that which constantly surrounds us, much less think about it seriously. It is only when we have acquired new habits of life and language, and with these habits new ways of assessing the world in which we live our lives, that we begin first to recognize and then to scrutinize what we once took for granted.

The water we swim in as North Americans, the environment that permeates every aspect of our daily lives, is a culture that has made "meeting needs" (some quite real, others fabricated) into what has literally become an "all-consuming" way of life. One recent study estimates that every man, woman, and child in the United States is exposed to 16,000 commercial messages and reminders every single day.[4] These indicators of our culture's passion for consumption inundate us, and yet, in what may be the most ironic twist of all, we are consuming more and enjoying it less. We are overwhelmed by the available choices and yet, at the end of the day, we wonder: is this all there is?

The principal problem is not the number of billboards, magazine advertisements, and television commercials we see every day, though they do constitute a symptom of our malaise. Nor is it just the sheer amount our society consumes, although this is indeed a problem. The ecological harm done by our society's habits of consumption, their damaging consequences to our health, our families, and our country, is also not our chief concern in this book, though those consequences are considerable. The real difficulty is that, as more than one pundit has noted, most of us no longer consume to live; we live to consume. Our lives are orchestrated around habits of consumption that no longer serve any higher purpose, but which have become ends in themselves, to be desired for their own sake. These habits in turn transform our relationships with other people, as friendships and even marriages are entertained around the question of meeting our personal needs.

It is almost impossible for most people in North America even to imagine any other way of living, much less to know why an alternative

4. Leslie Savan, *The Sponsored Life* (Philadelphia: Temple University Press, 1994), p. 1.

might be desirable. Our all-consuming way of life, as Rodney Clapp puts it, "appears to need no justification. To argue for or against it today, from almost anywhere in the world, seems to make about as much sense as arguing for or against the force of gravity or the wind in your face." Thinking of ourselves primarily as consumers strikes most people as "natural, a kind of cosmic given. It seems as inevitable and ineradicable a feature of the social landscape as the Rockies are of the geographical landscape."[5]

In such a context, talk of meeting needs, though it seems straightforward, in fact becomes a tricky business. To be sure, we humans are finite, mortal beings, and thus many things are needful. Each of us needs to eat and drink, wear clothes, and find shelter. God knows that we need such things, and Jesus' followers are to make sure their brothers and sisters within the household of faith are cared for, and to welcome those outside this fellowship of the Spirit (Matt. 6:32; Mark 10:28-30; Gal. 6:2). Humans are also made for life in the company of others: "Then the Lord God said, 'It is not good that the man should be alone; I will make him a helper as his partner'" (Gen. 2:18). Moreover, as creatures formed in the divine image, humans are made for life with God. St. Augustine puts it well when he prays at that start of his *Confessions:* "You have made us for yourself, and our heart is restless until it rests in you."[6] We are set apart from all other creatures by a desire, a longing for God that cannot be satisfied by anything or anyone else: "As a deer longs for flowing streams, so my soul longs for you, O God" (Ps. 42:1).

It is precisely at this point, however, that we need to move cautiously. In Scripture the need or longing for God has a social context and material content that routinely get trampled underfoot in a consumerist setting. In the Bible the desire for God is inextricably linked to a hunger and thirst for righteousness to be revealed at the coming of the rule of God (Matt. 5:6). Those who truly long for God thus desire to see "justice roll down like waters, and righteousness like an everflowing stream" (Amos 5:24). They know they must "eat and drink," but they also know that for it to go well with them they must

5. Rodney Clapp, "The Theology of Consumption and the Consumption of Theology," *The Consuming Passion: Christianity and the Consumer Culture,* ed. Rodney Clapp (Downers Grove, Ill.: InterVarsity Press, 1998), pp. 171-72.

6. Augustine, *Confessions,* I.1.

"do justice and righteousness" and "judge the cause of the poor and needy." As the prophet Jeremiah observes, "'Is not this to know me?' says the Lord" (Jer. 22:15-16). According to Jesus, our need for God is intimately tied up with the weightier matters of the law: justice, mercy, faithfulness (Matt. 23:23). Those who long for the God of Israel and of Jesus Christ do not receive a product to supplement their ordinary lives as consumers. Instead, they discover that their whole existence is to be re-created as they are drawn into a new set of relationships and a new identity.

In short, the beginning and end of the human longing for God is wrapped up with the mission of God and thus is inseparable from the desire to witness the coming of the all-encompassing reign of God. These linkages are invariably lost when the socially scripted role as self-interested consumer forms the center and ground of all value, the goal of all activities and relationships. In our time and place individuals hearken to whatever promises to provide them with the "choices" that will satisfy their self-directed appetites.

Unfortunately, the consuming spirit of our age has taken possession of most Christians in North America, and as a result they too find it difficult to imagine another way of life. They assume along with virtually everyone else that the primary purpose in life is to make choices that will satisfy their own interests and desires in every sphere allotted to them by the commercial institutions of society. Numbered among those spheres is religion. It thus seems natural to talk about our relationship with God as yet another lifestyle choice, another good or service for our enjoyment. Unless we are careful, "meeting needs" simply becomes another way of saying, "satisfying the customer."

If what we say seems overstated, consider how the notion of spirituality has changed over the centuries. In the New Testament, the Greek term *pneumatikos* ("spiritual") is intimately related to the Spirit who descended upon Jesus at his baptism (Mark 1:9-11) and who is the gift of the risen Lord to his followers (John 20:19-23; Acts 2:1-4). Those whom Paul describes as *pneumatikos* (e.g., 1 Cor. 2:15) are persons in whom the Spirit dwells and is at work. The spiritual thus does not pertain to extraordinary inner experiences unconnected to the world and people around us, but to the whole of life as engendered and empowered by the Spirit of God in the new pattern of life called the church. Spirituality thus denotes "a new pattern of personal growth taking

5

place in the community of those who have been sought out, converted and cherished by the risen Christ." It is not primarily concerned about certain intense feelings and affections, though these are invariably associated with the work of the Spirit, "but with the new network of communal relationship and perception that the presence of God makes possible for each spiritual person."[7]

In contrast, go to your nearest bookstore (it makes little difference whether it is Christian or general) and take a look at the religion shelves. What now passes for spirituality there is almost exclusively a private and inward matter, most often portrayed as a form of therapy designed to make one's life more fulfilling. A majority of those who call themselves Christians may retain a vague notion of religious identity, but as one author puts it, "their lives are distinctively secular. . . . Increasingly these nominal Christian . . . Americans embrace the heady hedonism and narcissism of popular culture and do not see that this contradicts biblical faith."[8] Indeed, this hedonistic and narcissistic culture transforms belief in God into yet another self-contained "experience."

We realize that such statements put us at odds with many well-meaning Christians across the theological spectrum. For these brothers and sisters, the notion that the love of God which moves the sun and other stars is ready, willing, and able to meet our individual needs is an essential truth of the gospel. And yet we shall try to persuade you that this way of approaching the gospel is deceptively seductive. No doubt some will be offended by this description. What could possibly be wrong about the church helping busy, on-the-go people cope with the stress and confusion of modern life, fashion more stable families, overcome every kind of abuse, enhance self-esteem, live more satisfying lives, and perhaps along the way make a positive difference in their local communities? Are we claiming, for example, that helping the victims and perpetrators of abuse is a bad thing? Of course not. Do we

---

7. Mark A. McIntosh, *Mystical Theology: The Integrity of Spirituality and Theology* (Malden, Mass.: Blackwell, 1998), pp. 6-7.

8. Vigen Guroian, *Ethics After Christendom: Toward an Ecclesial Christian Ethic* (Grand Rapids: Eerdmans, 1994), p. 89. For a more detailed examination of the ways market-driven conceptions of church life contradict the understanding of faith in Scripture, see Philip D. Kenneson and James L. Street, *Selling Out the Church: The Dangers of Church Marketing* (Nashville: Abingdon, 1997).

think that people are supposed to feel worthless? Perish the thought. Are functional families something to be avoided like the plague? Heavens no.

Why then do we regard the notion that the church exists to meet needs as somehow deceptive? It is not because we believe that God doesn't care whether we are unhealthy and unhappy, stressed out and without meaning in our lives. The problem rather lies in where our culture locates health, happiness, and meaning: namely, in the realm of private feelings and values rather than in the shared mission in which God's people participate. When Christians accept a consumerist culture's definition at face value, they look to the church primarily to provide them with the means to improve their private lives, enhance their self-esteem, give them a sense of purpose. Worship becomes a form of therapy whose sole aim is to improve the emotional state of individuals and to energize them for the week ahead. It is designed principally to make these individuals feel comfortable and to justify the style of life they find most satisfying. Quite frankly, such worship is little more than projection and wish fulfillment, "and all the unkind things psychologists have always tended to accuse religion of."[9]

How We Got Here

This seductive way of life did not just drop out of the heavens one day and land inside church sanctuaries. It represents the transformation of a well-established pattern in North American Christianity. For several decades now the church, especially in the United States, has looked to the wider culture for its sense of identity and purpose. In the past, this symbiosis of church and society took the form of a civic faith that found its home principally in the so-called mainline denominations. According to this understanding, writes Anthony Robinson, "The mission of the church is to ameliorate the human suffering of the city and to be the moral conscience of the community. The church, in this understanding, is a center of civic life, one that provides an avenue by which the most fortunate and powerful can be of help to the less fortu-

---

9. Rowan Williams, "The Dark Night," in *A Ray of Darkness* (Cambridge, Mass.: Cowley Publications, 1995), p. 80.

nate and least powerful. Such a church seeks to embody and carry religious meaning for the civil society."[10]

Once more, we are not trying to say that God wants Christians to ignore moral questions in the towns and cities where they live, or to turn a blind eye to the suffering of their neighbors. The problem again lies in the way modern culture defines such matters and, in the process, implicitly redefines the nature and mission of the church as well. The unspoken assumption that underwrote this understanding of the church and its mission was that the United States was a "Christian" society and nation. To be sure, our political system was not officially affiliated with any religious institution, and thus in that narrow sense was secular. However, what went virtually unnoticed for decades was that the formal separation of ecclesiastical and governmental institutions took place under the auspices of a social arrangement that sanctioned a moral and cultural identity between mainline Protestant Christianity and America. In such an arrangement, it was believed that politics could safely be assigned to a formally "secular" realm so long as the tacit ethos that informed public reason, morality, and politics were nominally Christian.

The understanding of the church as the moral conscience of the nation and a source of occasional benevolence still lingers alongside the captivity of God's mission for the therapeutic benefit of the community of Jesus' disciples. Over the last half of the twentieth century, however, the unifying ethos that informed this vision gradually began to fall apart, and all that remains are odd-shaped fragments and tattered remnants. The infamous "culture wars" between so-called "conservatives" and "liberals" are just one indication of a social fabric that is showing more than a few signs of wear and tear.

Although this civic faith has become polarized, the habit of looking to the wider world for a sense of identity and purpose is still firmly ingrained in Christianity across the theological spectrum. Ironically, this means that churches that cannot agree on the basics of doctrine or morals are drawn like moths to a flame to our culture's fascination with our feelings and thoughts. It is in the "inner" man, writes Ralph Waldo Emerson, that one finds "a new respect for the divinity in

---

10. Anthony B. Robinson, "The Making of a Post-Liberal," in *Good News in Exile: Three Pastors Offer a Hopeful Vision for the Church,* by Martin B. Copenhaver, Anthony B. Robinson, and William H. Willimon (Grand Rapids: Eerdmans, 1999), p. 16.

man."[11] In conservative and liberal churches alike, this fascination has stripped Christian piety away from its connection with a set of church practices and repackaged it in the form of self-care manuals and programs that contain techniques designed to be used in the privacy of one's own home, head, and heart. Such "spirituality" does not require any form of communal direction or oversight, recognition of any obligation or purpose outside one's skin, or a process that culminates in any meaningful sense of conversion.

In effect, the civic faith that was cultivated in traditional mainline Protestantism has been transformed into personalized "diet plans" for disembodied souls, complete with "before" and "after" testimonies. And this transformation has occurred across all denominational boundaries. It therefore comes as no surprise that, according to a recent report in the *Washington Post,* more and more Americans think it permissible to fashion their own god, one that is "a gentle twin of the one they grew up with. He is wise but soft-spoken, cheers them up when they're sad, laughs at their quirks. He is, most essentially, validating, like the greatest of friends . . . the God they choose is more like a best friend who has endless time for their needs, no matter how trivial."[12] What we, as discriminating shoppers of spiritual goods and services, finally want to know is, How will believing in this god improve my quality of life? Bottom line, what does this deity do for me?[13]

Facing Our Idolatry

The spirit of consumption thus holds captive the minds and bodies of Christians and non-Christians alike. The Bible has a name for such

---

11. Ralph Waldo Emerson, *Emerson's Essays* (New York: Harper Colophon Books, 1926), p. 56.

12. Hanna Rosin, "Beyond 2000: Many Shape Unique Religions at Home," *Washington Post,* January 17, 2000 (http://www.washingtonpost.com/wp-dyn/A58347-2000Jan17.html), p. A1.

13. Robert Jenson points out that the maxim beloved by most Protestants, that to know God is to know God's benefits, makes sense only when God's identity is already well established. In our context, says Jenson, this maxim "is plainly false and has been a disaster for the church." Robert Jenson, *Systematic Theology,* vol. 1, *The Triune God* (New York: Oxford University Press, 1997), p. 51n.68.

bondage: idolatry. The self-deceptive destructiveness of idolatry con-
sists of more than paying homage to the creature rather than the creator. The distinctively modern form of idol worship has taken our need
for material goods, for human companionship, and for God, and
turned them into the means for our captivity. The choices that consumers in North America regard as marks of their freedom from any
kind of slavery are themselves controlled by a vast social network of
production, distribution, exchange, and marketing. In other words,
when people make the meeting of their individual needs the center of
life, they have no choice but to play the game in the way dictated by the
"rulers and authorities" (Col. 1:16; 2:15) that supervise this network and
allocate their choices. They obey because these "spirits" promise to
meet their needs and to satisfy their wants and desires.

Whether for reasons of survival or to satisfy more self-indulgent
impulses, the spirits of our age take true necessities and use them as
the means to enslave us. We should not be surprised, then, when they
seek to domesticate the mission of God in the world in the same way.
As a result, when Christians uncritically adopt the marketplace language of meeting needs to talk about the gospel, they unwittingly re-
cast life with Christ into something individuals can relate to without
conversion, without moral or intellectual transformation, without the
lives of those who share God's creation with us. This language transforms the unfathomable mystery of God that rules over all things into
a neatly packaged deity custom-designed to satisfy our self-described
desires and appetites. And that is as much an idol as any sacred pillar,
pole, or statue fashioned from wood and clay (Deut. 12:2-3).

Though the particular way that the temptation to bow down to
idols comes to us at the start of the twenty-first century is new, the
challenge we face is quite ancient. The First Epistle of John warned believers in the first century that not every spirit that had gone out into
the world was from God, and thus they were to test the words of those
claiming to be prophets (1 John 4:1). It seems reasonable to expect that
the spirits of consumption that have indeed gone out "virtually" into
every corner of the world need to be tested (as does the vision of the
church and its mission offered to you in this book). How do we do
that? According to 1 John, the standard for such tests is the person and
work of Jesus, testified to in Scripture and commended by tradition
(1 John 4:2-3).

But which Jesus? In both the academy and popular culture we can find an almost infinite number of descriptions of Jesus: Jesus the revolutionary, Jesus the corporate manager, Jesus the therapist, Jesus the meek sacrifice, etc. Which picture is most faithful to the Scriptures and to the work of the Spirit in our midst today?

There are many places one could begin sketching a faithful account of Jesus, but we have decided to take our clue from the New Testament itself. The very first verse of Matthew's Gospel reads: "An account of the coming to be (literally, the 'genesis') of Jesus the Messiah, the son of David, the son of Abraham" (Matt. 1:1, author's trans.). Now some may argue that the fact that the New Testament canon begins with the Gospel of Matthew is mere coincidence and that we should not assign any special significance to this particular verse being the first statement we come across. But it seems to us that Matthew's gospel was accorded first place in the canon to make a point: that to understand Jesus we need to go back to beginnings of the people of Israel and then trace the story all the way through. We invite you to follow this path with us, for along it lies a faithful and fruitful vision of the *missio Dei,* the mission of God, about which the apostle Paul says: "All this is from God, who reconciled us to himself through Christ, and has given us the ministry of reconciliation" (2 Cor. 5:18).

God's Mission in the People of Israel

As the New Testament texts themselves make abundantly clear, the mission to redeem creation that God undertakes in history did not originate either with Jesus or with the apostolic witnesses to his life, death, and resurrection. "Do not think that I have come to abolish the law or the prophets," Jesus said to the crowd on the mount. "I have come not to abolish but to fulfill" (Matt. 5:17). When he uttered these words, God's redemptive work had been underway for centuries, beginning with the election of Abraham and his descendents, to whom God said, "All the families of the earth shall be blessed in you and in your offspring" (Gen. 28:14). At Mt. Sinai the Lord God of Israel reaffirmed through Moses the promise to Abraham's offspring, "You shall be for me a priestly kingdom and a holy nation" (Exod. 19:6).

These promises and covenants are the basis for the gospel of Jesus

Christ. Paul confirms this relationship in a statement addressed to Gentile believers: "So then, remember that you Gentiles by birth . . . were at that time without Christ, being aliens from the commonwealth of Israel, and strangers to the covenants of promise, having no hope and without God in the world. But now in Christ Jesus you who once were far off have been brought near by the blood of Christ" (Eph. 2:11-13). The church, by virtue of its inclusion into the covenants and commonwealth of Israel through Christ's passion and resurrection, also shares in God's purpose for summoning Abraham and Sarah in the first place — to bless all the families of the earth. In other words, the community of Jesus' followers exists primarily to participate in God's work in the world, not for its own sake.

By the time that Jesus came onto the scene announcing the drawing near of God's reign (Mark 1:14-15), the people of Israel had been laboring for centuries to make sense of what had happened to them over their long history with God, and particularly after their expulsion from the promised land in the sixth century BCE. In Babylon, Egypt, Asia Minor, and Roman-occupied Galilee and Judea, the covenants God had made with their ancestors seemed remote, their promises unfulfilled. And yet the Jews did not abandon the ways of their forebears. Instead they sought to cultivate a way of life that could cope with the harsh realities of exile and dispersion while at the same time striving to remain faithful to the God of Abraham and Sarah, Miriam and Moses, Deborah and David, Jeremiah and Huldah. In the course of this tenuous task they found themselves faced with many difficult questions.

A host of tensions and ambiguities permeated life in exile and dispersion. In their synagogues and in the rebuilt Temple in Jerusalem, Jews worshiped the God of their ancestors and prayed with the psalmist, "The Lord, the Most High, is awesome, a great king over all the earth. . . . Sing praises to God, sing praises; sing praises to our King, sing praises. For God is the king of all the earth; sing praises with a psalm" (Ps. 47:2, 6-7). They declared that there was no king but God, whose dominion over the creation admitted no rivals and no partners. And yet everywhere they looked in their daily lives they saw something very different. Most of them lived in foreign lands with strange and idolatrous customs, and though some had returned to the land of Israel, even there they were slaves in their own land, its produce going to foreign kings (Neh. 9:36-37). Moreover, a vast array of worldly powers and authorities each claimed privileges and prerogatives the Jews reserved for God alone. In short, God's return to Zion in triumph, as the prophets had promised (Isa. 52:8; Ezek. 43:1-2, 4-5, 7; Hag. 2:6-9), had not yet materialized.

Whether in dispersion or in the Promised Land, then, the Jewish people found themselves hard pressed between competing allegiances. There was the exclusive and all-encompassing claim of the God of Abraham, the God of Isaac, and the God of Jacob on them: "Hear, O Israel: The Lord is our God, the Lord alone. You shall love the Lord your God with all your heart, and with all your soul, and with all your might" (Deut. 6:4-5). God's claim on this people touched on every aspect of life — eating, drinking, the apportionment of property, the administration of justice, and the like. Monotheism was not an abstract idea about how many gods there were or what God was like, but "always a polemical statement directed outwards against the pagan nations."[14]

This does not mean that beliefs and doctrines were incidental to this common life by any stretch of the imagination. But convictions are like threads in a garment; once they are removed from that piece of cloth, they lose all pattern and purpose. For Jews in the post-exilic era, the ideas they held, like monotheism and idolatry, were "a shorthand way of articulating the points of pressure, tension, and conflict between different actual communities, specifically, Jews and pagans."[15] The grasp of the truth that arises from Israel's covenant with God "is never a truth beyond history, subsisting in any kind of Platonic heaven. Neither is it a universal morality, as so many modern Jews have thought. . . . Judaism is nothing without the Jewish people. Only this people can bring this truth off, almost like a joke that a particular performer can bring to life but when told by others falls flat."[16]

Loyalty to the God of their ancestors thus demanded of this people a certain way of life that would distinguish them from the ways of the peoples in whose midst they lived. Yet at the same time they were faced, as all people are, with the daily necessities of building houses, planting

14. N. T. Wright, *Who Was Jesus?* (Grand Rapids: Eerdmans, 1993), p. 49.

15. N. T. Wright, *The Climax of the Covenant* (Minneapolis: Fortress Press, 1992), p. 122.

16. Michael Wyschogrod, *The Body of Faith: God in the People Israel* (San Francisco: Harper & Row, 1983), p. 28.

gardens, marrying and giving in marriage, raising sons and daughters, and, yes, consuming to live, and they had to do so among these same peoples. Moreover, they had to attend to the task of securing not just their own well-being, but also the peace of the place where they lived. "Seek the welfare of the city where I have sent you into exile," God told them through the prophet Jeremiah, "and pray to the Lord on its behalf, for in its welfare you will find your welfare" (Jer. 29:7). The pressure to conform was constantly pressing in on them from all sides.

Over the centuries, Israel cultivated this difficult art of living between competing interests and loyalties, and it has proven to be a precarious way of life, full of pitfalls and detours, and yet this people has persevered for over two millennia. They labored in various ways and with varying degrees of success to carve out a form of life befitting their identity and vocation as God's chosen people, while learning to cope with the established ways of their hosts. They developed practices and institutions that gave shape and direction to their lives and enabled them to remain faithful to God in foreign lands.

One practice in particular that stands out is the way they attended to their present circumstances in light of their past, that is, in terms of a story that was not over. They gathered on the Sabbath in local synagogues to read from a common set of texts generated by their ancestors' experiences with God. Indeed, it was due in no small measure to the fact that the Jews were compelled to learn time and again in new circumstances what it meant to be God's in-between people that the biblical canon gradually took shape. "Living as strangers in a strange land," write Martin Copenhaver, Anthony Robinson, and William Willimon, "Israel's very identity as a people was threatened, so they read and listened to stories to remind them of who they were and where their true home was."[17]

They discovered through these stories that the presence and activity of their God could only be discerned in terms of a constantly unfolding pattern of events that moved them continuously toward an open future. Over the centuries, they came to know history, not as simply one disconnected thing after another, but as contingent events linked purposefully together within a dramatic narrative that drove mysteriously yet inexorably toward a fitting climax — the reign of

17. Copenhaver, Robinson, and Willimon, *Good News in Exile*, p. 34.

God! The action was focused first and foremost on a God who would not abandon the world to its own futile resources and thereby abdicate sovereignty over heaven and earth. Creation was always turning away from its source and head, but God would not leave it to its own devices. Instead, God was constantly disrupting humankind's self-devised plans and strategies. According to these stories, the only way human beings could ever hope to discern the meaning and goal of such a world was by acknowledging God's claim to sovereignty over every aspect of it.

Moreover, as the plot of history moved toward its dramatic conclusion, with all kinds of twists and turns, reversals and repetitions, God's people discovered that time and again they were right in the thick of things, that they themselves were the point of divine incursion into the affairs of humans. God had indeed chosen this people, not to satisfy their every desire while ignoring the needs of other nations, but so that through their life together God's mission of redeeming heaven and earth might have an earthly dwelling place. The continued existence of Israel as a nation in dispersion, which by all rights should have disappeared from the face of the earth centuries ago, remains a crucial testimony to the enduring sense and significance of this story, not simply for itself, but for all peoples.

In the Midst of the Storm:
God's Mission in a Fallen World

Israel's priestly mission, however, was not an easy one. On more than a few occasions it involved no little suffering, as Michael Wyschogrod puts it, "for the sanctification of God's name."[18] Time and again the people found themselves in the midst of a violent storm, so to speak, with God in the thick of it, stirring up the nations. "As I looked," writes the prophet Ezekiel, "a stormy wind came out of the north: a great cloud with brightness around it and fire flashing forth continually. . . . This was the appearance of the likeness of the glory of the Lord" (Ezek. 1:4, 28). The image of a storm, found throughout the Old Testament, is particularly well suited for depicting what happens to the group of

18. Wyschogrod, *The Body of Faith,* p. 24.

15

people who are summoned to share God's mission to redeem a violent and idolatrous creation. Warm moist air coming in off the water collides with cool dry air from the hills, generating a storm front that triggers strong winds, heavy rains, and damaging hail. In their aftermath the land is scarred, as are the lives of the people who endure them. This indeed was the experience of the people of Israel. Throughout their history they were compelled to strive with God and other human beings as if encompassed by a storm, and they continued to do so, and in their striving they endured, and the name of God was made known throughout the nations (cf. Gen. 32:28; Ezek. 36:22-32).

Not that the Jews were the only ones who suffered from the searing winds that plague a fallen world. From the Scriptures they learned about the curse of violence, rebellion, and death that extended from the time human beings first began to walk the earth. This reign of sin and corruption was like the stagnant dome of high pressure that hovers over the parched earth during the sweltering days of summer. The entire world languished under the oppressive rule of powers and authorities that literally saps the life out of every living thing. But the Jews also learned from these same stories that the God who had called all things into being would not leave these powers and authorities to their own mischievous designs and devices but was determined to bless the work of creation. And they had been chosen to be that people through whom God's blessing would come to the rest of the world.

When the first signs of God's mission to bless all the families of the earth appeared on the distant horizon, however, they were barely distinguishable even to the most discerning of eyes, like "a little cloud no bigger than a person's hand" (1 Kings 18:44), scarcely worth a second thought. Abraham and Sarah, a man and woman without so much as a single heir, were summoned to leave their ancestral home and journey toward an uncertain future and an unknown place. By all appearances they were destined for a life of obscure anonymity, and yet their lives and those of their descendents would be anything but that. So it is that, as Gerhard Lohfink puts it, "God begins in a small way, at one single place in the world. There must be a place, visible, tangible, where the salvation of the world can begin: that is, where the world becomes what it is supposed to be according to God's plan. Beginning at that place, the new thing can spread abroad, but not through persuasion, not through indoctrination, not through violence. Everyone must have the opportunity to come and see. All must have the chance to behold and test this new thing."[19]

From the fragile and fallible faithfulness of this couple, a small group of people emerged over the course of several generations. As the refreshing, life-giving breath of God mingled with the searing blasts of death and rebellion, however, Ezekiel's storm cloud also began to boil up on the horizon. The first faint rumbling of thunder came wafting across the arid wasteland when Abraham and Sarah's descendents, now a small group of peasants and herdsmen, suffered under the brutal hand of oppression and slavery. Their deliverer from bondage in Egypt was identified by a strange name, which we may paraphrase as, "You will come to know me only as you follow me."[20] As the name testifies, this people was once again compelled to undertake a journey into an uncertain future and toward an unknown place, with only the instructions of a covenant to hold the fragile band together. As we noted above, the purpose of this covenant was that there might be in this world "a priestly kingdom and a holy nation" (Exod. 19:6). Through this covenant Israel's mission as God's in-between people, first articulated in the covenant with Abraham, was reconfirmed.

Even the land to which God led them was an in-between place, situated at the junction of Europe, Asia, and Africa. From the rise of the great ancient civilizations in Egypt, Asia, and Asia Minor until today, the great empires of the world have fought for control of this land. Hittites, Egyptians, Philistines, Assyrians, Babylonians, Persians, Hellenists, Romans, Muslims, Crusaders, Europeans, and Americans have all sought to control this tiny corridor that connects three continents. If God wanted to protect the chosen people of Israel, keep them safe from harm, one could not have chosen a worse place to put them. If, on the other hand, God wanted a people to come into contact with all the nations of the world, there are few places on this planet more suited for the purpose.

Through the wind and rain that followed the exodus from Egypt and the establishment of a nation, God's mission for and with Israel re-

---

19. Gerhard Lohfink, *Does God Need the Church? Toward a Theology of the People of God,* trans. Linda M. Maloney (Collegeville, Minn.: Michael Glazier, 1999), p. 27.

20. See James Wm. McClendon, Jr., *Systematic Theology,* vol. 1, *Ethics* (Nashville: Abingdon, 1986), p. 182.

mained unchanged. When the nation became a monarchy, the prophets served as the advocates and interpreters of God's sovereignty over against the pretensions of the royal and priestly families. Contrary to popular opinion, these prophetic figures were not solitary religious geniuses who set themselves over against the institutionalized power of canonical texts, dogmatic traditions, priestly hierarchies, and rote liturgies. Rather they kept alive in Israel both the ancient memory *and* the contemporary meaning of divine kingship, and along the way they helped refine the picture of the God Israel served and of themselves as the chosen people. "Thus says the Lord," said the prophets, continuing the story of Israel's only true sovereign. That sovereign, the prophets insisted, demands justice from those in power, advocates the cause of the poor and oppressed, and invites all toward that future country where "they shall all sit under their own vines and under their own fig trees, and no one shall make them afraid; for the mouth of the Lord of hosts has spoken" (Mic. 4:4).

The storm clouds hanging over Israel gathered strength when the Jewish people were taken into exile in Babylon in 587 BCE and then were dispersed among the nations. The exiles longed to see God return to Jerusalem and thus sanctify his name (see Ezek. 36:22-23, Ps. 79:9), but their hopes remained unfulfilled while the intensity and frequency of these storms increased. The apocalyptic sections of the Old Testament, especially the book of Daniel, extended the prophetic oracles of judgment and redemption that gave direction and content to the people's understanding of God's rule and set them in a new, radical frame. The whole cosmos, not just the people of Israel and their immediate enemies, now stood under God's sovereign judgment. Israel's hopes for the coming of the reign of God could no longer be accommodated by the world as it existed; it could only come about after the patterns and structures that order day-to-day life had been completely transformed. These visions and dreams served both to intensify and to focus the missional impulse that drives history for God's people.

The apocalyptic writings that influenced most directly the mission of Jesus and the early church divided history into the exile of the present age (in Hebrew, *ha-ʿolam hazeh*) and the age to come *(ha-ʿolam habaʾ)*. During the present age the wicked flourish, while God's people languish under the rule of idolatrous powers that claim for themselves what belongs to God alone. In the age to come, all creatures will witness the restoration of God's sovereignty and the vindication of Israel and righteous Gentiles — in short, a new creation. Because the present world cannot contain the promise made on behalf of all nations to this in-between people, there arose the expectation that God would bring the present order of the world to an end. Extraordinary phenomena — eclipses, earthquakes, and floods — were sometimes regarded as portents of what we would metaphorically call "earth-shattering events."[21] But it is important to realize that such events, including the ones that were expected to come as the climax of God's restoration of Israel, "remained within (what we think of as) the this-worldly ambit."[22]

Another important idea developed in close proximity with these apocalyptic expectations in post-exilic Judaism. A messianic figure that would bring about the triumph of God at the end of the present age entered the story. The initial impetus for this idea emerged from the struggle between the proponents of uniting the tribes of Israel under a king and those who advocated for the idea that God alone was king. This crisis led eventually to the prophets designating the human king of Israel, the one who follows the Lord (cf. 1 Sam. 12:14), God's "anointed."[23] By the time of the first century CE, the idea could be found in several varieties of Jewish thought, though certainly there was no standard or uniform use of the term "messiah." Indeed, the gospel story itself substantially revises this concept even while employing it extensively.[24]

---

21. Wright, *Who Was Jesus?*, p. 55.

22. N. T. Wright, *The New Testament and the People of God* (Minneapolis: Fortress Press, 1992), pp. 298-99. The expectation that the present world order would pass away did not include the end of the space-time world. Wright adds that "it was the Stoics, not the first-century Jews, who characteristically believed that world would be dissolved in fire" (p. 285).

23. Martin Buber, *Kingship of God,* 3rd ed., trans. Richard Scheimann (New York: Harper & Row, 1967; Atlantic Highlands, N.J.: Humanities Press International, 1990), p. 162.

24. For a survey of messianic expectations leading up to the first century CE, see Wright, *New Testament,* pp. xiv, 307-20 and N. T. Wright, *Christian Origins and the Question of God,* vol. 2, *Jesus and the Victory of God* (Minneapolis: Fortress, 1996), pp. 481-89. For an excellent discussion of how the idea of a messiah has been treated in Jewish circles, see Gershom Scholem, *The Messianic Idea in Judaism* (New York: Schocken Books, 1971).

According to the story of Israel, then, God refuses to leave the world to its brokenness and violence, but time and again disrupts the "normal" causal sequence of history with stormy signs of the coming kingdom. God chose this people to be the medium through which this disruption takes place, so that God could reclaim rightful dominion over a world presently ruled by death and sin. What is promised to the chosen people, then, is not that God comes to meet their needs, but that through their participation in God's mission in the world all the families of the earth might be blessed. In the Scriptures of Israel, the promises of God are always related to Israel's mission to be a priestly nation. As a result, the chosen people found themselves time and again in an unenviable place — in between a sovereign yet merciful God and a rebellious creation.

The Storm Intensifies: God's Mission in the Work of Jesus

God's call to Israel to be a holy nation and a priestly people sets the communal and historical context out of which the gospel emerges. It is this story, recounted in the scriptures, that informs Jesus' proclamation to his fellow Israelites, "The time is fulfilled, and the kingdom of God has come near; repent, and believe in the good news" (Mark 1:15). The New Testament consistently depicts the body of Christ as the first fruits of a new creation in the midst of the old. This means, among other things, that Israel's existence as an in-between people is taken up by Jesus and his followers, albeit in a new mode. But what does this mode consist of precisely?

In his first letter to the Corinthians, the apostle Paul recounts some of the events that took place when the God of Israel delivered the chosen people from their bondage in Egypt and then cared for them as they made their way through the wilderness. He notes that though God was faithful to them, most of them were not faithful in turn, slipping instead into patterns of idolatry and the immorality and indulgence that invariably follow the worship of idols. Paul then makes a fascinating comment that sums up quite well what we would contend is a main theme of his understanding of the church's mission: "These things happened to them to serve as an example, and they were written down to instruct us, *on whom the ends of the ages have met*" (I Cor. 10:11, author's translation).[25]

As that group of people on whom the two ages have met, Christ's followers live much as did the saints of Israel who came before them, not hidden away in a safe place, removed from harm's way. They are instead gathered together by God to live under constant threat of a powerful thunderstorm (to continue this image from the Old Testament), generated by the meeting of the ends of the ages in and through their participation in the crucified and risen Lord. This event divides the present age, over which sin and death have the final say in human affairs, from the time to come, when God will be all in all, creation itself will be liberated from its bondage to decay, and life rather than death will have the final word for all creatures. As André Trocmé puts it, "Jesus is the central event of history, because *de facto* man is not the same after Jesus Christ as before."[26]

Think about it this way: time contracts in the ministry, death, and resurrection of Jesus, allowing the life and harmony of God's eternal kingdom to confront concretely the death and conflict of history. But this contraction of time that allowed the present age to come into contact with the age to come, thus forming an "apocalyptic storm front" in the midst of history, did not "re-expand," so to speak, with the resurrection and ascension of Jesus. Instead, it continues to manifest itself in the life of the church, through which "the wisdom of God in its rich variety might now be made known to the rulers and authorities in the heavenly places" (Eph. 3:10). That is to say, *in, through,* and *with* the church the meeting of the two ages, decisively marked by Christ's ministry, passion, and ascension, is extended beyond the confines of first-century Palestine. The line that marks the boundary between the present age and the age to come, drawn by God's redemptive work in Christ, cuts straight through the church and through each baptized member of his body.

---

25. As Richard Hays notes, the two-age schema that is central to Paul's understanding of last things is obscured by English translations that treat his plural ("the ends of the ages") as a singular "the end of the ages," or the verb "to meet" as "to come." Richard B. Hays, *The Moral Vision of the New Testament: Community, Cross, New Creation: A Contemporary Introduction to New Testament Ethics* (New York: HarperCollins, 1996), pp. 19-21, 56n.14.

26. André Trocmé, *Jesus and the Nonviolent Revolution,* trans. Michael H. Shank and Marlin E. Miller (Scottdale, Penn.: Herald Press, 1973), p. 11.

God forms this body with persons gathered from every tribe and nation, language and culture (Rev. 5:9), to be its living members, not for their own sakes, but for the sake of a world that even in its violence and rebellion God has never stopped cherishing. These followers of Jesus do not simply find themselves passive bystanders to what the mission of God accomplishes for the redemption of the world. That mission continues with the living sacrifice of the bodies of these disciples (Rom. 12:1) in the power of the Spirit, thus suspending them together with Jesus between a world destined to pass away and a new heaven and a new earth that will never pass away.

Simply put, the Holy Spirit puts this company of fragile and fallible saints squarely on the line drawn between the two ages by Jesus, where life is never boring, frequently precarious, and many times downright dangerous. "For while we live," Paul tells the saints in Corinth, "we are always being given up to death for Jesus' sake, so that the life of Jesus may be made visible in our mortal flesh" (2 Cor. 4:11). This understanding of Jesus and the church in the New Testament represents a further development of the ideas and images of Jewish apocalypticism. Paul tells the Corinthians that for those who are in Christ, this new creation has already come into view: "So if anyone is in Christ, there is *a new creation:* everything old has passed away; see, everything has become new" (2 Cor. 5:17).

These links to Jewish apocalypticism, and more generally to the practices and dispositions of first-century Judaism, can be traced to Jesus himself. The New Testament consistently presents Jesus, and Jesus seems to have understood himself, as a living recapitulation of Israel's history and mission. Through his obedience and faithfulness to God, Jesus did not merely copy the history of Israel but realized it afresh in his own life. Everything that Jesus did and said represented not only Israel's past but also what Israel would become in the future through God's mighty consummating works. In every strand of the biblical witness, the account of who Jesus is and what he does is patterned either explicitly or implicitly around the life, the suffering, and especially the mission of the Jewish people.

Consider, for example, the following passage in Mark's Gospel. Jesus tells his disciples, "Truly I tell you, there is no one who has left house or brothers or sisters or mother or father or children or fields, for my sake and for the sake of the good news, who will not receive a hundredfold now in this age — houses, brothers and sisters, mothers and children, and fields *with persecutions* — and in the age to come eternal life" (Mark 10:29-30). Not only does the imagery of two ages appear prominently in this passage, so does the recognition that belonging to Christ's circle of friends in this age brings with it two things: a foretaste of the blessings of the messianic age in the form of shared practices and resources, *and* the sort of trouble that comes with belonging to a group that refuses to play by the established rules of the game.

As this passage makes clear, the Christian community is also constituted by this apocalyptic connection with the story of the chosen people. Life with Christ is "the life of itinerant Israel over again, with the same trials and temptations . . . but the Christian now knows that what was being rehearsed in a preliminary way in the history of Israel was the life of Christ with his faithful followers." In the community of Jesus, says E. J. Tinsley, the Christian life "is bound to be a series of variations on the theme of the 'Way' of . . . Israel as it has been summed up for them in Christ."[27] The lives of these first Christians testified to all that happened when this living recapitulation of the Way of Israel drew decisively near in the ministry of Jesus. In particular, they bore witness to its conflict with the established authorities and powers that culminated in his crucifixion at the hands of the Jewish and Roman authorities. In the early church, therefore, the cross most directly embodied the apocalyptic motifs that lie at the heart of the gospel.

In the New Testament, the brutal and unjust execution of Jesus of Nazareth was the decisive point of confrontation between the oppressive and sinful conditions of the present age and the life and harmony of the age to come. The crucifixion thus combines several interwoven layers of meaning. At its most basic level, it was a free act of sacrifice offered by Jesus to God for the sake of God's people and thus marks God's eschatological intrusion into the world on its behalf. So Paul writes in the salutation to his letter to the Galatians that the Lord Jesus Christ "gave himself for our sins to set us free from the present evil age, according to the will of our God and Father" (Gal. 1:4). But even as a sacrificial act, the cross does not stand by itself. It is depicted as the culmination of a life lived wholly out of obedience to God. In the famous

---

27. E. J. Tinsley, *The Imitation of God in Christ* (Philadelphia: Westminster, 1960), p. 157.

Let the same mind be in you that was in Christ Jesus,

who, though he was in the form of God,
    did not regard equality with God
    as something to be exploited,
but emptied himself,
    taking the form of a slave,
    being born in human likeness.
And being found in human form,
    he humbled himself
    and became obedient to the point of death —
    even death on a cross.

Therefore God also highly exalted him
    and gave him the name
    that is above every name,
so that at the name of Jesus
    every knee should bend,
    in heaven and on earth and under the earth,
and every tongue should confess
    that Jesus Christ is Lord,
    to the glory of God the Father.

Therefore, my beloved, just as you have always obeyed me, not only in my presence, but much more now in my absence, work out your own salvation with fear and trembling; for it is God who is at work in you, enabling you both to will and to work for his good pleasure.

Philippians 2:5-13

christological hymn in Paul's letter to the Philippians, we read that Jesus "humbled himself and became obedient to the point of death — even death on a cross" (Phil. 2:8).

In a variety of ways, the New Testament describes the cross as necessary for the redemption of the world,[28] but not to satisfy some sense of divine honor or justice. Nowhere in its pages do we find a courtroom scene in which God is the righteous judge, Christ the defendant, and his death the vicarious payment of a divinely imposed penalty. The cross is necessary because of the kind of world we have made for ourselves, a world bent not toward God but toward violence and death. Crucifixion is what happens when someone is faithful to God rather than to the rulers of this world. Atonement occurs in turn because of God's faithfulness to Jesus' obedience. Paul thus describes the cross as a triumph over the rulers and powers of this present age (Col. 2:15). By accepting the cross, Jesus demonstrated that he was free from the rebellious deceptions of a world that thinks that the creature rather than the creator determines the order and end of all things.

Simply put, Jesus refused to "paint by the numbers" in a fallen world; rather, he colored outside the lines, beginning a masterpiece that God calls the new creation. In this basic sense, then, the cross of Christ was a unique and unrepeatable event, accomplishing for our sake what we could never accomplish for ourselves. It was that crucial moment in space and time where the life-and-death struggle for the destiny of the world was definitively and decisively joined.[29] And yet, the New Testament also speaks of the cross as the paradigm for our participation in the life and mission of Christ. This mission comes from the God who has never stopped overturning the humanly contrived order of things and who now does so through the church's communal life of faithfulness to the faithfulness displayed by Jesus.

Again, the hymn in the second chapter of Philippians can help us. Its description of Jesus' death as the culmination of a life lived wholly out of obedience to God is introduced with the admonition: "Let the same mind be in you as was in Christ Jesus," and it concludes with the

28. In the story of the two disciples making their way to Emmaus, for example, the resurrected Jesus appears to them and says to them, "Was it not necessary that the Messiah should suffer these things and then enter into his glory?" (Luke 24:26).

29. To speak about his suffering and death as a moral example of how one ought to live and die for one's fellow human beings thus fails to do justice to what he accomplished.

reminder, "It is God who is at work in you, enabling you both to will and to work for his good pleasure" (Phil. 2:5, 13).[30] Similarly, the anonymous epistle to the Hebrews declares that it was fitting that God,

> for whom and through whom all things exist, in bringing many children to glory, should make the pioneer of their salvation perfect through sufferings. . . . Since, therefore, the children share flesh and blood, [Christ] himself likewise shared the same things, so that through death he might destroy the one who has the power of death, that is, the devil, and free those who all their lives were held in slavery by the fear of death. . . . Therefore Jesus also suffered outside the city gate in order to sanctify the people by his own blood. Let us then go to him outside the camp and bear the abuse he endured (Heb. 2:10, 14-15; 13:12-13).

In these passages, the cross signifies a way of life lived wholly out of obedience to God, thus establishing a pattern to be repeated *within* and *by* the communal body of Christ. As Paul puts it in his letter to the Romans, the righteousness of God is revealed through the faith of Christ for our own life of faith (Rom. 1:17; 3:26). The storm front generated by the confrontation between the two ages, decisively established by the events of Jesus' life, now cuts straight through the church, sweeping up each and every member of Christ's body into its maelstrom. Christ's followers thus frame the temporal interval between Pentecost and Parousia within which all creation is now set. Within this interval, writes Paul, they become in Christ the righteousness of God (2 Cor. 5:21) and thus anticipate for the sake of the world the reconciliation and healing of creation that will take place at the end of this age.

We need to remember, however, that this location is not one of repose; it is at the center of the storm. The church's participation in God's mission and ministry of reconciliation (2 Cor. 5:18-19) also makes it heir to the enmity that the present age harbors for the ways of the world to come. "Blessed are those who are persecuted for righteousness' sake," says Jesus, "for theirs is the kingdom of heaven. Blessed are you when people revile you and persecute you and utter all kinds of evil against you falsely on my account" (Matt. 5:10-11). Paul likewise commends the saints in Thessalonica because they "became imitators of us

---

30. In the Greek, the pronoun "you" in these verses is always second person plural.

> So if anyone is in Christ, there is a new creation: everything old has passed away; see, everything has become new! All this is from God, who reconciled us to himself through Christ, and has given us the ministry of reconciliation; that is, in Christ God was reconciling the world to himself, not counting their trespasses against them, and entrusting the message of reconciliation to us. So we are ambassadors for Christ, since God is making his appeal through us; we entreat you on behalf of Christ, be reconciled to God. For our sake he made him to be sin who knew no sin, so that in him we might become the righteousness of God.
>
> 2 Corinthians 5:17-21

and of the Lord, for in spite of persecution you received the word with joy inspired by the Holy Spirit, so that you became an example to all the believers in Macedonia and in Achaia" (1 Thess. 1:6-7). Again in the second chapter of 1 Thessalonians, Paul reminds his readers, "For you, brothers and sisters, became imitators of the churches of God in Christ Jesus that are in Judea, for you suffered the same things from your own compatriots as they did from the Jews" (1 Thess. 2:14).

As central as the cross is to the gospel entrusted to Jesus' followers by God, however, it never stands by itself, and this is the best news of all, for in God life and not death has the final word for creation. The early Christians thus celebrated the resurrection as God's vindication of the way of Christ signified by the cross. With the ascension of the risen Lord to the right hand of God, they boldly and joyfully declared that the world was no longer the same, that it had definitively crossed the threshold of the age to come. The rulers and authorities of this present age, though not directly acknowledging Christ's lordship, had been decisively defeated and brought under his sovereignty, and thus they were the unwitting servants of God's final (though still future) triumph.

The communal practices and traits of character that bound together this motley mob of misfits and malcontents in a new style of life were thus a tangible sign to the world about them that God's everlasting reign was now making its way to the ends of the earth in the power of the Holy Spirit. The messianic rule of God in Christ established the goal toward which all things tend, and it also set the limits for the exercise of power by all worldly authorities. In and through this small group of people, everything in the created order, all life, was "now, at once, immediately confronted with a claim that is non-negotiable in the sense that in the end God will irrefutably be — God."[31] Their confession of Christ's lordship — celebrated in weekly gatherings and lived out daily in a holy life of communal solidarity and hospitality to the stranger — bore witness to the world that the end toward which all creation was moving was not determined by those whom this age calls powerful, but by the one who gathers together all things in heaven and on earth in the crucified Messiah of Israel (Eph. 1:10).

The visibility of this fellowship was crucial, for though the triumph of God over death on Easter morning signaled that this new era was at hand, the "end" was not yet. Paul's description of the church as living between the times typifies the struggle of the New Testament authors to find appropriate ways to depict this overlap between two ages and two social orders, for in appearance most things went on pretty much as they had before. Babies were born, goods were bought and sold, the priests and scribes continued to gather at the Temple, the Romans looked to expand their empire further, and death still exercised its terrible dominion over the created order. The summons of Jesus in the Sermon on the Mount for his followers to be salt and light (Matt. 5:13-16) draws metaphorically upon two different senses of the body to drive home the same point: that they were to manifest the coming reign of God to a world that was withering away.

God's Mission in the Church

As we have seen, the mission of the church is the same as its Lord's mission: to put the bodies of its members on the line between the two ages on behalf of him who lived and died for the sake of the world. But when churches talk of "meeting needs" and "satisfying our customers," they miss both the letter and the spirit of Paul's admonition to the

31. McClendon, *Systematic Theology*, vol. 2, *Doctrine*, p. 66.

saints in Rome: "Do not be conformed to this world, but be transformed by the renewing of your minds, so that you may discern what is the will of God — what is good and acceptable and perfect" (Rom. 12:2). In our day and time it is the language of the market that governs the ways of the world in Paul's sense of that term. The vocabulary of commerce and the syntax of consumption not only distort our relationship with God and thus with each other, they also miscast the church in the role of retail vendor, trading in spiritual goods and services. Thus the market conforms the members of Christ's body to its ways precisely at the point where the risen Lord summons them to be transformed.

At the beginning of this chapter, we promised that we would lay out a different vision of what the God revealed in Jesus Christ is up to in the world. We believe this vision is the one that is most faithful to the Scriptures in our place and time. We have only just begun to sketch the outlines of that vision. In the next chapter, we shall begin to fill in some of the details.

2

ALLEGIANCE

Participating in God's Intentions

As the first chapter has shown, North American Christianity has difficulty understanding and living out the gospel because the church has become all too captive to a consumerist mindset that focuses attention on meeting needs, on personal growth, and on personal choice. This captivity of viewpoint has largely obscured the biblical picture of a God whose mission is to reclaim and restore the whole creation. In North America, we find it difficult to understand and to embrace the biblical vision of an apocalyptic "storm front" where God dynamically and tumultuously engages creation. We prefer to keep God in the private sphere, confined to matters of personal growth and wholeness. We are less comfortable with the broader vision of God's presence and activity in the world outside our private lives.

This misguided longing for a God who only meets our needs also skews our vision for the church. The problem is that, in North America, the church has become largely a vendor of religious services, rather than "that group of people on whom the two ages have met" (p. 21). Families "shop" for churches in the same way that they shop for groceries, each family looking for a congregation that will match its style and needs most closely. Some churches become "niche marketers," targeting specific populations with carefully packaged messages designed to address their needs and concerns. Other churches show little interest in reaching out to the unchurched people around them. Instead, they focus on caring for their own members with great diligence, in order to assure that they won't move on to the greener pastures of a more comfortably equipped sanctuary or a more winsome preacher down the road. In both cases, however, what goes unquestioned is that the church — especially its paid staff — exists for the purpose of meeting the needs of its members and/or its community. There are churches that intuitively resist these postures, but they struggle to find authentic ways to sustain their corporate lives in a consumerist culture that seems to undermine their discipleship at every turn.

But the problem goes deeper still. It would be challenging enough merely to attempt to confront the myriad ways in which we North American Christians have domesticated the biblical God, worshiping instead a more comfortable deity better suited to our own felt needs. It would be challenging enough simply to seek to refocus the life of the church away from dispensing religious goods and services and toward being the body of Christ. But these are not our only challenges. We also must confront the ways in which these ills of the North American church have infected our theology, particularly our understanding of God's salvation.

Salvation is the focus of this chapter: The eclipse of the biblical God discussed in the first chapter has led also to an eclipse of the biblical understanding of what it means to receive salvation. In the Bible, talk about salvation refers primarily to God and God's victory over all the powers that resist and distort God's gracious purposes for the world. The Bible sees life as a great struggle between life and death, between sin and righteousness, between faithfulness and rebellion, between peace and violence. The good news of salvation is the announcement that God wins: God's life is stronger than death. God's righteousness is deeper than human sin. God's faithfulness outlasts human rebellion. God's peace is more enduring than human violence. For North Americans, by contrast, salvation is more focused upon how God *meets our needs*. It's about overcoming our guilt, solving our problems, discovering meaning in our existence, feeling included and loved, and overcoming the threat of our death and the death of those we love — all of course with God's help.

What's wrong with the idea that God meets our needs? Isn't the Bible full of stories where God heals, rescues, enlivens, delights, feeds, and cares for people? Of course it is. But here's the problem: We North Americans tend to think of meeting our needs as not just one good thing among many other aspects to life. We tend to think of meeting our needs as the central purpose of our lives. We regard it as a kind of moral mandate that precedes all other duties and responsibilities we might have. It's what gives our lives their meaning at the deepest level. We have accepted the notion that the great drama of human life is the challenge to get one's needs met.

We think this way because we tend to identify our humanity at its core with a set of needs that must be met. The clearest exposition of this is found in the writings of Abraham Maslow. He held that human beings are characterized by a hierarchy of needs. At the base of the hierarchy are what he called the "lower-level needs," things humans need in order to survive and achieve basic health — air, food, safety, etc. Once these needs are met, human beings engage progressively higher sets of needs, finally culminating in the need for self-actualization. Life acquires its energy and dynamism from our relentless attempts to meet these needs.[1]

The reason this image of human life acquires such power in North American life is that it is the image of our humanity that is reinforced thousands of times each day through the culture of advertising. Daily we are bombarded with images, phrases, music, and sensations that invite us to consider those things that we need or desire, and to exert our energies toward the satisfaction of those desires and needs. In essence, North American understandings of what it means to be human are deeply shaped by the market. We are *trained* to see ourselves first and foremost as consumers with needs to be met.

Such training begins at a very early age. The largest marketer of toys in the world is the McDonald's corporation. They know that if they acquire "brand loyalty" in preschoolers, they will have customers for life. Soft drink companies spend huge sums of money to win exclusive contracts with school systems, so that their brands will be constantly in front of impressionable young people. To these examples could be added dozens more illustrating the dramatic expansion of the market's role in our culture. Markets are nothing if not efficient, and their expanded cultural role has brought along with it their enormously efficient and effective capacity to direct our culture toward the pursuit of needs and desires.

---

1. Abraham H. Maslow, *Toward a Psychology of Being*, 2nd ed. (New York: Van Nostrand Rheinhold, 1968).

What is lacking in this view of humanity? Glaringly absent is any understanding of a purpose for human life that extends beyond ourselves and the gratification of our own needs and desires. The problem is not that meeting needs is wrong; it's that when meeting needs moves to the center of our lives, the result is self-absorption and narcissism. Genuine spiritual growth is difficult to achieve until this posture of self-absorption is confronted and addressed.

What the gospel offers, by contrast, is the opportunity to be drawn into something larger than ourselves — into God's overflowing love that moves out in ever-widening circles, embracing the whole of creation. The gospel sees our humanity not in terms of needs to be met, but in terms of capacities and gifts to be offered in God's gracious service. We are created not to consume but to know God, not merely to meet our own needs but to participate in God's life and mission.

In the final analysis, the biblical understanding of salvation is not merely that our lives will be set right again at last. The biblical understanding of salvation is that our lives become swept up into something larger and greater than ourselves, into God's purposes for the world. In other words, the receiving of salvation and the call to mission are not to be conceived sequentially, as if one followed the other (first salvation, then grateful obedience in mission). Rather, to receive salvation *is* to be called into something larger and greater than we are, to be invited to participate in God's saving purpose and plan for the world. That is why the gospel is primarily about God, and only secondarily about us.

But our culture is relentless in its tendency to twist the biblical, missional understanding of the gospel into a consumerist one. The tragic result has been the proliferation in America of passively oriented churches, preoccupied with their own survival and the care of their own members and struggling to discover a sense of transcendence and the presence of God. By contrast, the gospel calls into existence churches whose fundamental identity is that of a people called to participate in God's mission, caught up into a reality greater than themselves, invited to bear witness to the world of a new way of being human in God's presence. There is much that the North American church has to learn from the biblical understanding of the gospel.

A Closer Look at the Gospel: It's About God!

It comes as no surprise, considering this context, that we North American Christians tend to see the gospel as a message directed to our needs. We think this way because such ways of thinking flow directly from the implicit understanding of humanity that is constantly thrown at us from every direction. A more detailed exploration of the gospel in the Bible will help pinpoint more precisely those ways in which North American Christians need to sharpen our grasp on the gospel and its implications for our lives.

Gather a dozen Christians into a room and ask them the question, "What is the gospel?" The likelihood is that you will receive a dozen different answers. Some Christians will speak about forgiveness of sins, entering into a personal relationship with God by faith in Jesus Christ, and the gift of eternal life. They may add to this the incorporation of the believer into the body of Christ — the new humanity begun in Christ. Other Christians will speak of liberation from oppression and injustice, of reconciliation, or of the restoration of creation. Still others will speak of the power of the Holy Spirit, healing, miracles, freedom from demonic powers, and of a joy so intense that words simply cannot express it. Still other Christians will speak of strength in the midst of weakness, courage in the face of suffering, comfort, peace, and the capacity to face death unafraid.

All these answers are attempts to explain what is *good* about the good news. They are a diverse set of answers, and their diversity helps explain the widely divergent forms in which North American Christianity expresses itself: evangelicals, mainlines, Pentecostals, middle-class suburban congregations, store-front revival chapels — the list goes on and on. Yet despite the great diversity among these different understandings of the gospel, there is a striking common theme that unites almost all of them. They all speak about the gospel in terms of its impact upon human life or upon the creation as a whole. The gospel is defined by the way it transforms our lives and our world. Of course, the character, location, and scope of the transformations envisioned vary widely — from personal to corporate to cosmic, from private and interior to social and economic — but these are merely variations on the same theme: the gospel is about something good that happens to us.

When we turn to the Bible, however, we discover a different perspective. The Bible doesn't speak about the gospel primarily in terms of its impact upon human life. Now this is a tricky distinction, and we need to be precise here. Certainly, the New Testament proclaims the gospel as something that has profound significance for human life. Yet it does not speak about the gospel *primarily* in those terms. If you survey the data in the New Testament, a very clear pattern emerges. The focus falls not so much on what we experience, but on what God has done and is doing in the world. When Jesus speaks about the gospel, he uses the term primarily to refer to the kingdom of God or the reign of God.[2] When the rest of the New Testament writers speak about the gospel, they use the term primarily to refer to what God has done in Jesus.[3] There are times, of course, when the New Testament speaks about the gospel in terms of its saving impact upon this world,[4] but that is not the primary accent in the biblical materials. The primary emphasis in the use of the term "gospel" is on a narrative that announces what God has done in Christ.

The gospel is first of all about God's faithfulness, about God's triumph over death, and about God's new purposes for the world that are revealed in the life, death, and resurrection of Jesus of Nazareth. These biblical patterns distinguish themselves in subtle but important ways from our North American ways of speaking about the gospel. Whereas we tend to speak about the gospel in terms of its impact upon our lives, the Bible tends to speak of the gospel as a revelation of who God is and what God is doing and has done in the world.

Why has the focus of our understanding of the gospel shifted in this way, from a focus on God to a focus upon our own experience? One could point to many reasons. Ever since the Enlightenment, western culture has found it difficult to articulate a clear and compelling vision of God's relationship to the world. In reaction to the Enlightenment, the theological stream of pietism has tended to confine the presence and action of God to the interior subjectivities of individual believers: "You ask me how I know he lives? He lives within my heart!" By contrast, another reaction to the Enlightenment, the more rationalisti-

2. See, for example, Matt. 4:23; 9:35; 24:14; Mark 1:14-15; Luke 4:43; 8:1; 16:16.

3. See, for example, Acts 5:42; 8:12; 8:35; 10:36; 11:20; Rom. 15:20; 16:25; 1 Cor. 15:1ff.; 2 Cor. 2:12; 4:4; 9:13; Gal. 1:7; Phil. 1:27; 1 Thess. 3:2; 2 Thess. 1:8; 2 Tim. 2:8.

4. E.g., Rom. 1:16; Eph. 1:13; Col. 1:5ff.; 2 Tim. 1:10.

cally inclined stream of deism, identified God only as creator and moral agent and removed God's presence and action almost entirely from the sphere of human history. God was compared to a watchmaker, who created the world and then simply let it run on its own. Another theological stream, made up of currents such as the social gospel movement and liberation theology, has identified God's presence and action in history almost entirely with various social movements toward progress, liberation, equality, and the betterment of human society and creation as a whole. The result has been a strong ethical vision, but some difficulty distinguishing between God's action and human efforts. Some strands of neo-orthodoxy, by contrast, identified God's presence and activity so exclusively with the historic revelation of Jesus Christ that any talk of God's ongoing action in the historical process became extremely problematic.

Given this diversity of ideas we have to deal with, no wonder it is often easier for us to talk about our experiences than it is to talk about God, easier to talk about the gospel's impact upon us than about the God who is revealed in the gospel. Our experience is tangible and concrete; God is mysterious, elusive, and transcendent. Since we find ourselves in a scientific, rationalistic, technologically driven society that leaves little room for God, it is simpler and more accessible to shift the focus to human experience instead. At least when we are talking about human experience, we can still tap into humanity's basic longings for God — longings that can still provide a starting point for speaking of God's saving purpose revealed in the gospel.

We confront here both the "push" and the "pull" that tends to throw us off in our thinking about the gospel. On the one hand, the market orientation of our culture pushes us toward thinking about our own identities primarily as consumers with needs to be met, rather than as gifted participants in God's gracious action in the world. On the other hand, the secular, scientific, rationalistic, and technological character of our society pulls us away from talk about God and directs our attention instead to our own more accessible experience. These two forces exercise a powerful influence over the way we North Americans think about the gospel, making it hard for us to hear the biblical resonances clearly.

The Kingdom of God:
Participating in God's Community

If we are to retain clarity of vision amidst this push and pull, we need a rekindled imagination that is grounded more deeply in Scripture. In particular, we need to grasp the vision implicit in Jesus' proclamation of the kingdom of God. As we explore this concept, we shall discover that human experience and divine action are not set off against each other in the kingdom of God, but rather are brought into dynamic relation. It is precisely this dynamic relationship — the capacity to see ourselves as participants in God's mission in the world — that we most sorely need in our understanding of the gospel.

In order to understand the kingdom of God, we first need to understand the role of the king in the ancient world. This requires an exercise of the imagination, since kingship represents a social structure vastly different from our own experience and assumes a whole pattern of relationships quite alien to our culture. To put it in simplest terms, in the ancient world the king is the richest person around. He commands most of the resources in the country. The king's power, however, comes essentially from generosity. That is, the king gives to others (especially to other nobles) and expects allegiance (both personal and financial) in return. The nobility, in turn, make land available to peasants and expect in return that the peasants will offer their allegiance (both personal and financial) to the nobles. This reciprocity of generosity and allegiance represents the fundamental "contract" that defines social life in the ancient world.

It is very clear that Israel saw its relationship with God in this framework — indeed, in Israel's view, God's kingship is the paradigm that all earthly monarchies only vaguely reflect. God showed generosity by rescuing the people from Egypt and then gave them the law, which codified exactly the form of allegiance that was expected from the people, in response to God's kindness and generosity. Biblical research has clearly established the link between the covenant at Sinai and other "suzerainty treaties" that were common in the ancient world.

The New Testament also picks up the same conceptual structure. It is evident, for example, in the parable of the marriage feast in Matthew 22:1-14. Here the king throws a wedding feast for his son, and the invitees refuse to come. The king responds by burning their city. To our modern sensibilities, this seems harsh and capricious. But in the ancient world it made perfect sense. The refusal to accept the generosity of an invitation was tantamount to insurrection. It was a refusal to enter into the relationship of generosity and allegiance that marked the basic structure of the ancient world. To refuse the generosity of the king was to set oneself as the enemy of the king.

This interaction between generosity and allegiance not only binds the people to their king; it also binds them to one another. One sees this most clearly in the Lord's Prayer, where we are instructed to ask for God to forgive us (i.e., to show us generosity) only to the extent that we have acted in the same way to those who have wronged us. The Bible uses the terms "steadfast love" *(chesed)* and "faithfulness" *(emeth)* to grasp these twin values that define social life as God intends it, both in our relationship to God and to each other.

Our modern blind spots appear with greater clarity when viewed against this biblical background. In our capitalist society, most transactions are impersonal, rather than personal. Goods and services are exchanged for money, not for allegiance. Consequently, when we hear the good news of God's gracious generosity, we readily respond by accepting the gift, but rarely do we understand ourselves to be obligated by the gift to ties of allegiance to God and to God's people. Salvation thus becomes a matter of having one's needs met, rather than being drawn into what God is doing in the world.

But the kingdom of God, as it is announced in the New Testament, is focused centrally upon this notion of being drawn together into God's new society, initiated through God's presence and activity in the world. People were called to a new citizenship in this kingdom[5] and were urged to see themselves as part of a new household of God.[6] Jew and Gentile alike were being drawn into a newly constituted people of God, the new "Israel of God."[7] The early Christians believed that this new religious/social reality was the direct result of God's new action in Jesus. But when early Christians reflected upon what God had done in Christ and its implications for their own lives, they thought about this within the social frameworks and assumptions of their day. For them,

5. Phil. 1:27; 3:20.
6. Eph. 2:19; 1 Tim. 3:15; 1 Peter 4:17.
7. Gal. 6:16.

39

the gospel of Christ was basically an announcement of a new social context — a new kingdom — into which their lives were placed by God's action. This reality is marked essentially by God's generosity (grace) and human trust and allegiance (faith).

However, as mission scholar George Hunsberger has pointed out, there is a striking discrepancy between the way in which Jesus spoke of the reign of God and the way it is often spoken of today. Often today you hear people speak of "building" the kingdom or reign of God. The New Testament never uses that verb and instead calls us to "receive" the reign of God as a child (Mark 10:15; Luke 18:17), to "inherit" the kingdom (Matt. 25:34; 1 Cor. 6:9-10; 15:50; Gal. 5:21), and to "enter" the reign of God (Matt. 5:20; 7:21; 18:3; 19:23-24; Mark 9:47; 10:23-25).[8] All these verbs cohere with the basic picture of kingship we have been describing. One "receives" a kingdom by accepting the generosity of the king whose initiative establishes the social order. By "inheriting" a kingdom, one becomes a member of a household (hence an heir) — again, part of a social order that has the king at its center. One "enters" the kingdom by entering into the communally shaped form of life that is defined by the king's action.

Hence, God's kingdom is not and cannot be established by human efforts. Jesus' teaching is all about God's reign, brought about by God's action, in fulfillment of God's purposes. It is not something we build. We only receive it, inherit, it, and enter it. Our lives are drawn into what God is doing. The parables echo this perspective over and over. The reign of God is like a man who accidentally discovers a huge treasure, hidden in a field; he did nothing to earn it — he just discovers it (Matt. 13:44). The reign of God is like the tiny, inconsequential mustard seed that grows into a huge shrub, or even a tree (Mark 4:30-32; Matt 13:31-32; Luke 13:18-19). It is like seeds sown in all kinds of strange places, most of which bear remarkable fruit (Mark 4:3-8; Matt. 13:3-8). It is like the thief that breaks in at an unexpected hour (Matt. 24:43-44; Luke 12:39-40), or the bridegroom who comes after everyone has given up on him (Matt. 25:1-13), or the vineyard owner who arrives after folks believe that they have stolen his vineyard and done away with him (Mark 12:1-11; Matt. 21:33-44; Luke 20:9-18). In all of these parables, what is striking is the re-

---

8. Darrell L. Guder, ed., *Missional Church: A Vision for the Sending of the Church in North America* (Grand Rapids: Eerdmans, 1998), pp. 93-97.

markable absence of human effort or initiative, even the reversal of human efforts. The emphasis falls entirely on the mysterious and surprising advent and growth of the reign of God, quite apart from or beyond, even against, human efforts. In the kingdom of God, the initiative always belongs to God.

Of course, the reign of God requires a human response, which may involve great effort. The merchant sells all he has to buy the pearl of great price (Matt. 13:45-46). The unjust steward runs around changing his master's credit slips when he knows he will be fired (Luke 16:1-8). Yet the human response the parables call for is always a matter of aligning oneself with the coming reign of God — receiving and entering that reign in grateful allegiance, not bringing it into existence. Even where the emphasis falls on the necessity of a response and decisive action, the parables consistently portray such actions as responses to the much larger reality of God's gracious action. The one constant throughout the parables is that the reign of God catches people by surprise.

So, for Jesus, hearing the gospel entails recognizing, entering, and receiving this surprising reign of God, in which God's presence and action intrude mysteriously and unexpectedly into our lives and invite us to participate in something greater than ourselves, greater than what we could accomplish on our own. The announcement of the gospel is an invitation to be caught up in God's surprisingly new way of working in the world, where the poor sit down at rich banquet tables, the sinners and the pious eat together, where old divisions come crashing down, where the sick are healed, demons are cast out, the proud are humbled, fearful hearts are given fresh courage, and the powerful are left on the sidelines. It is this sense of God's reign and God's purposes that has led many missiologists to speak of the centrality of the *missio Dei* — the mission of God — rather than our mission for God.

Mark 1 as a Test Case

With this more general background, we turn to a closer look at the beginning of the Gospel of Mark, in order to explore more fully what it means to receive and enter God's kingdom. What difference does it make when we read the Bible and understand the gospel from this per-

The beginning of the good news of Jesus Christ, the Son of God. As it is written in the prophet Isaiah,

> "See, I am sending my messenger ahead of you,
>   who will prepare your way;
> the voice of one crying out in the wilderness:
>   'Prepare the way of the Lord,
>   make his paths straight.'"

John the baptizer appeared in the wilderness, proclaiming a baptism of repentance for the forgiveness of sins. And people from the whole Judean countryside and all the people of Jerusalem were going out to him, and were baptized by him in the river Jordan, confessing their sins.

Mark 1:1-5

spective? The opening of this Gospel provides a helpful place to discover how these themes appear in the ministry of Jesus.

Mark begins his Gospel with these words: "The beginning of the good news [or *gospel*] of Jesus Christ, the Son of God." He continues by citing from two Old Testament texts:

See, I am sending my messenger ahead of you,
who will prepare your way;
the voice of one crying out in the wilderness:
"Prepare the way of the Lord, make his paths straight."

For Mark, the "messenger" is clearly John the baptizer, and the "you" is Jesus. When the prophecy speaks of "your way," this is not the way by which humans reach God, but rather the way by which Jesus, the divine messenger, is to come to human beings: it is *the Lord's* "paths" that are to be made "straight" (1:3). The next verse goes on to say, "John the baptizer appeared in the wilderness, proclaiming a baptism of repentance for the forgiveness of sins" (1:4). The repentance, baptism, and forgiveness that John calls for here are portrayed entirely as part of the preparatory process for the Lord's coming. It is because the Lord is coming — and because the Lord's coming will define a radically new social reality — that repentance, forgiveness, and cleansing are both necessary and possible. There is a new kingdom and a new king, and people must bring their lives into alignment with this reality. All this was to take place "in the wilderness," that place where long ago the Hebrew people were delivered from bondage and first learned what it meant to be a *people* in whose presence God dwelled.

In our contemporary North American context, we characteristically misread this passage. We tend to understand ourselves as individuals, not as embedded in larger social and religious contexts. We therefore construe John the baptizer's call as a summons to a form of personal holiness expressed as repentance. This personal holiness is the necessary precondition of a proper personal encounter with Jesus. We lose, therefore, the profoundly social context of this passage — its evocations of Israel of old, as well as the character of John's ministry as a movement itself.

Our misunderstanding of this passage is revealed in a characteristic problem pondered in this text: Why does Jesus undergo John's baptism, if he does not need the forgiveness of sins (cf. Matt. 3:14)? The traditional answer is that Jesus' baptism is done vicariously, on behalf of sinful humanity.[9] Yet Mark offers no indicators in the text that suggest this vicarious interpretation. Even Matthew, who is more explicit about this problem, states that the baptism is necessary and proper "to fulfill all righteousness" (Matt. 3:15). The righteousness spoken of here is not one's personal righteousness, but the proper form of life for God's people as a whole, in order to prepare for God's gracious presence and activity in new ways. In John's baptism, individual repentance, cleansing, and forgiveness is a process of incorporating people into a movement, a new people who await God's presence and action in fresh ways, just as Israel did in the wilderness long ago. Jesus undergoes this baptism because he sees himself as part of this movement, part of this new people that God is calling forth.

9. John Calvin writes, "For in general, the reason for Christ's undergoing baptism was to offer His father full obedience, while the particular reason was to consecrate baptism in His own body, that it might be common between Him and us." *Calvin's New Testament Commentaries,* vol. 1., trans. A. W. Morrison (Grand Rapids: Eerdmans, 1972), p. 130.

What emerges quite clearly from this quick overview of the opening of Mark is that John's proclamation of the gospel is essentially an invitation to his hearers to participate in God's mission to the world. God is doing a new thing, coming to Israel to be its savior. The proper response of the people (a response that Jesus himself adopts) is to receive this generosity and to bring their lives into allegiance to God in this new way that God is present and active in the world. All this stands in some tension with our characteristically North American ways of reading this text — readings that tend to focus on the individual while ignoring the ways in which John's message calls for our participation.

Other Biblical Images for Salvation as Participation in God's Life

At root, then, we believe that if North Americans are to grasp the gospel in all its biblical truth and power, we need to rediscover the ways in which the gospel comes to us as *an invitation to participate in God's life*. A quick survey of important biblical images bears this out. In the Gospel according to Mark, immediately after Jesus undergoes baptism and begins to announce the reign of God, he also calls the first disciples (Mark 1:14-20). The announcement of the reign of God and the calling of disciples are two sides of the same coin. If God is indeed creating a new reality in which people are called to participate, then such invitations must be extended. It is noteworthy, in this regard, that *discipleship* continues to be the root metaphor employed by Matthew in his gospel for Christian life in general. In the Great Commission at the end of Matthew (28:16-20), the New Testament's most ringing summons to missionary activity for generations of Christians, the main verb employed is "to make disciples."

Yet we are not to construe discipleship only as one's personal relationship with Jesus. The disciples are sent out by Jesus to preach, teach, and heal. Jesus repeatedly instructs them on the quality and character of their relationships with each other. In calling disciples, Jesus is establishing a new community. In fact, many scholars suggest that Jesus' calling of twelve disciples implies that Jesus saw these disciples as the beginning of the new people of God, the fulfillment of the twelve tribes of Israel.

These same participatory and social themes characterize other root images in the New Testament. In John 17, Jesus prays that his followers "will be one" (17:20-21), and that the love between the Father and the Son might also reside within the new community (17:26). This love expresses itself first of all as mutual loyalty — love for one another (13:34-35). In John 15, where Jesus uses the familiar image of the vine and the branches, the same reality is in view. Jesus' disciples abide (remain) in Jesus by keeping his commandments: "If you keep my commandments, you will abide in my love, just as I have kept my Father's commandments and abide in his love" (15:10). The next portion of the chapter goes on to explicate exactly what "keeping Jesus' commandments" involves: "This is my commandment, that you love one another as I have loved you" (15:12). Thus the fourth Gospel joins the other three in its emphasis on the social and participatory character of Jesus' ministry and the reign of God that he announces. The gospel not only announces a gift to be received; it announces a new gracious social reality established by this generosity, in which people are invited to participate — a social reality marked by the vivid and life-giving presence and activity of the triune God.

In the letters of Paul, the same themes occur, this time surrounding Paul's language of being "in Christ." It is clear that Paul conceives our union with Christ to be at the center of his understanding of the gospel. It is crucial to understand that Paul believes Christ to be not only *representative,* but also *incorporative.* Christ died and rose *representing* us, on our behalf. That is not only a gift we receive; it is also a reality into which we are *incorporated.* That is, the death and resurrection of Christ on our behalf not only accomplishes something for us (as if we were not involved), but makes us participants in that death and resurrection.

In 1 Corinthians 15:22, both Adam and Christ are presented as persons in whose lives the destiny of others is implicated: "For as all die in Adam, so all will be made alive in Christ." The same reality is addressed in Romans 6, related to baptism. Baptism is presented here as incorporation into Christ's experience shared in the life of the church: "Do you not know that all of us who have been baptized into Christ Jesus were baptized into his death? Therefore we have been buried with him by baptism into death, so that, just as Christ was raised from the dead by the glory of the Father, so we too might walk in newness of life" (Rom.

45

6:3-4). The gift of justification and forgiveness of sins incorporates us into the body of Christ, so that "we too might walk in newness of life."

This same understanding of Christ's incorporative work comes through clearly in the later Pauline literature, especially the letter to the Ephesians, where the writer speaks of the plan revealed in Christ, "a plan for the fullness of time, to gather up all things in him, things in heaven and things on earth" (Eph. 1:10). Participation in Christ is the goal and purpose of God's entire redemptive plan. But exactly what does this participation in Christ look and feel like? What does it mean, concretely, to be "in Christ"? Again, the quote from Ephesians begins to point the way to the answer. God's entire redemptive purpose is to "gather up" all things in Christ. The image is of adding up, drawing together discrete items until they form a single unity. That's why, later in chapter two, the writer goes on to speak of how the gentiles are now incorporated into the people of God by faith (Eph. 2:11-22).

Here we see the crucial connection between Paul the missionary and Paul the theologian. Paul's entire life was devoted to itinerant missionary service, and he started new congregations all over the Roman Empire. He did this because he was convinced that the new reality revealed in Christ is essentially incorporative in character. The reign of God that Jesus announced pointed to a new way in which God was present in the midst of a new people, where old distinctions between Jew and Greek, slave and free, male and female were abolished (Gal. 3:28).

The characteristic ethical passion that enlivens Paul's letters flows from this basic conviction: Paul's converts must learn how to live in the new reality in Christ into which they have been drawn. They must learn new patterns of conflict resolution and peacemaking appropriate for life in Christ (Rom. 14). They must learn to distinguish the movement of the Spirit in their midst from other spirits that might lead them astray (1 Cor. 12:3). They must discover how their lives fit together in Christ into a larger reality (1 Cor. 12:4-31). They must discern how to live at the edge of the apocalyptic storm front unfolding by God's action, with one foot in "this age" and the other foot in the "age to come." Paul's instructions regarding work, marriage, lawsuits, wealth, and the like are all shaped by this concern. Receiving the gospel and being "in Christ" means participating in a new form of community — a community whose practices and lifestyle must be learned.

One other key image that should be mentioned is that of *inheritance.* Both Paul and those who followed him speak frequently of our receiving salvation as an inheritance (1 Cor. 6:9-10; 15:50; Gal. 3:18, 29; 4:7; 5:21; Eph. 1:14, 18; 5:5; Col. 3:24; Titus 3:7). Because of our consumerist mindset, we almost instinctively think of inheritance in terms of receiving a gracious and unearned gift. However, in both Paul's thinking and in the New Testament more generally, receiving an inheritance is most centrally connected with becoming a full member of a household. This is clear, for example, in Galatians 4:7: "So you are no longer a slave but a child [literally, *a son* — a male heir], and if a child [son], then also an heir, through God." Because the ancient world thought of households as the basic social unit for all of life, becoming an heir of God meant becoming part of a basic social unit defined by God at its center.[10]

This emphasis on heirs as participants in a social group makes sense in light of the Old Testament as well. There, the concept of inheritance often refers to receiving the Promised Land, for example in Genesis 15:7, Deuteronomy 30:5, and Numbers 34:2. In these passages, the meaning is clear that to receive God's inheritance is to enter into the land and to become part of the people who live in God's presence. Inheritance means participating in the people of God, not merely receiving a gift.

This survey of images could easily be extended, but the general point is clear. The gospel announces a shared reality in which people are called to participate. This reality is based upon God's gracious generosity, expressed in forgiveness of sins, reconciliation with God and with each other, the empowering of the Holy Spirit, healing, and eternal life. Yet all these blessings are the characteristics and qualities of the shared reality that the biblical writers believed was breaking into history in the life of the people of God, the church. Further, these blessings were never conceived as only for the church itself. The church is always envisioned as the "first fruits" of God's redemptive purpose, which is directed toward the whole of creation (e.g., 2 Thess. 2:13; James 1:18; Rev. 14:4). Participation and mission are the key characteristics of the reign of God announced in the gospel.

10. On the nature of households as the basic social unit, cf. this comment from Aristotle, who discusses households in the context of his discussion of politics and the state: "Now that it is clear what are the components of the state, we have first of all to discuss household management; for every state is composed of households . . ." (Pol. 1.1253b).

At one level, this survey of biblical themes may seem rather simple and self-evident. Yet our contention that the gospel points to an essentially social and participatory reality represents a significantly different emphasis from the one we find in classical Protestantism. The churches of the Reformation have characteristically spoken of the gospel in terms of justification by faith. The gospel, in this context, refers to the good news of God's work in Christ. Through the perfect sacrifice of Christ, our sins are atoned for and we are reconciled to God through faith in Christ, quite apart from any righteousness or good works on our part.[11]

How does our emphasis differ from this approach? We certainly do not reject the doctrine of justification by faith, nor its significance for the life of the church. Yet we believe that the characteristic Reformational focus upon justification by faith has, in our North American context, led to a confusion of means and ends. Justification by faith has come to be understood as the purpose for which Christ died and rose again, the end and goal of God's entire saving purpose. By extension, the central human problem is construed to be guilt, and the central human resistance to the gospel is construed to be the establishing of our own righteousness, rather than the receiving of God's righteousness in Christ as a free gift. Salvation is therefore achieved precisely at the moment of individual repentance and faith, when one is justified. Everything that follows after this in the Christian life is simply working out the implications of this climactic event.

When the gospel is understood in this way, the social and participatory dimensions of the gospel necessarily recede into the background. Particularly in North America, the receiving of the gift of justification is no longer clearly understood as an invitation to participate in God's life amidst God's people. In our American revivalist tradition, church membership is an experience subsequent to conversion, a step required primarily to sustain and preserve the new grace into which one has entered. By contrast, we would argue that justification and forgiveness are the necessary preparation for participating in God's life and mission. They are the means to a greater end, not the end in itself.

11. See, for example, "The Gospel of Jesus Christ: An Evangelical Celebration," *Christianity Today* 43, no. 7 (14 June 1999): 49.

Galatians as a Test Case

But it is not enough merely to assert such things. Let us consider Paul's letter to the Galatians as a test case. Here, if anywhere, the link is strongest between the gospel and the doctrine of justification by faith. Perhaps we can best focus the issue this way: If the gospel is about being drawn into participating in God's life and mission, and not centrally about justification by faith rather than works of the law, then why does Paul believe that the Galatians are turning to a different gospel (Gal. 1:6) by observing works of the law, such as circumcision (Gal. 2:7-14)? Doesn't this sound as if justification by faith rather than works of the law is at the heart of the gospel?

Justification by faith is at the center of the traditional understanding of Galatians, which unfolds as follows: The most important human question is how we can be accepted (justified) in God's sight. Until Christ, the only way this could even be attempted was through the keeping of the law. Yet such an experience is doomed to failure. Galatians 2:16b states, "No one will be justified by the works of the law." The good news is that God has provided a way for humans to be accepted by God — the sacrifice of Christ. This sacrificial understanding of Christ's death is therefore crucial to the gospel (Gal. 2:21). The death of Christ pays the penalty for our sins (our inability to keep the law) and enables us to escape judgment and to have the hope of eternal life.

There are several problems with this traditional understanding. First, nowhere in Galatians does Paul speak about keeping the law as a means of being acceptable before God. More importantly, there is no evidence that Jews in general thought this way about the law. There is no evidence that any first-century Jews believed that they were acceptable to God only if they kept the whole law. Jews believed that all fail from time to time, but that God is merciful and forgives the transgressions of the penitent.

This observation has led a number of recent scholars to suggest that justification (being made righteous) is more about one's status as a member of the people of God than about one's acceptance before God. Frank Matera's summary of recent research is illuminating:

> While the traditional perspective on Paul is good theology in
> light of the sixteenth century debates about justification, it is

I am astonished that you are so quickly deserting the one who called you in the grace of Christ and are turning to a different gospel — not that there is another gospel, but there are some who are confusing you and want to pervert the gospel of Christ. But even if we or an angel from heaven should proclaim to you a gospel contrary to what we proclaimed to you, let that one be accursed! . . .

When they saw that I had been entrusted with the gospel for the uncircumcised, just as Peter had been entrusted with the gospel for the circumcised (for he who worked through Peter making him an apostle to the circumcised also worked through me in sending me to the Gentiles), and when James and Cephas and John, who were acknowledged pillars, recognized the grace that had been given to me, they gave to Barnabas and me the right hand of fellowship, agreeing that we should go to the Gentiles and they to the circumcised. They asked only one thing, that we remember the poor, which was actually what I was eager to do.

But when Cephas came to Antioch, I opposed him to his face, because he stood self-condemned; for until certain people came from James, he used to eat with the Gentiles. But after they came, he drew back and kept himself separate for fear of the circumcision faction. And the other Jews joined him in this hypocrisy, so that even Barnabas was led astray by their hypocrisy. But when I saw that they were not acting consistently with the truth of the gospel, I said to Cephas before them all, "If you, though a Jew, live like a Gentile and not like a Jew, how can you compel the Gentiles to live like Jews?"

Galatians 1:6-8; 2:7-14

not exactly what Paul is talking about in Galatians, according to the new perspective. As Dunn and others have noted, the problem in Galatia was more social in nature, albeit a problem with profound theological implications. . . . "Works of the law," then, is not Paul's code word for works righteousness or a legalism by which individuals seek to justify themselves before God. In Galatians, it refers to certain specific works of the law that would, if adopted, identify the Galatians as having embraced a Jewish way of life, presumably to share more fully in the blessings of the Messiah. Paul's primary problem in Galatia, then, was not legalistic but social in nature. How should two communities that believe in Christ relate to each other? Is it necessary for one to adopt the cultural patterns of the other in order to form one community and stand in the correct covenant relationship to God, that is, to be justified?[12]

Other recent research on Galatians also suggests results consistent with our overall point. The gospel, including the doctrine of justification, points to the reign of God, a dynamic reality into which people are called to participate. It is an essentially social reality, energized by God's presence, which marks the "apocalyptic storm front" distinguishing the present age from the age that is coming. It is not addressed primarily to meeting needs, nor does it point to a reality that is primarily individual, private, subjective, or personal. The gospel is about the coming of God's reign, and its call upon us is a call to participation.

Conclusion

How then do we proclaim the gospel in North America? If our discussion in this chapter is at all accurate, it suggests that we face a specific challenge. North Americans will readily understand and embrace the notion that God is gracious to us and will meet our needs. Such a message fits well with our basic assumptions about what it means to be human at all. However, North Americans will have considerably more difficulty understanding how God's generosity is an invitation to

---

12. Matera, "Galatians in Perspective," *Interpretation* 54, no. 3 (July 2000): 236-37.

participate in God's life, as it finds expression in the community of people who are related to God and to one another through the bonds of generosity and allegiance. They also will have more difficulty sensing the organic link between receiving God's mercy and being bound to God and to God's people in ties of allegiance and faithfulness.

Yet if the church is to recover its missional identity, these themes must be clearly sounded, understood, and embraced. As it was during the Reformation, so it is today. A clear understanding of the gospel and a clear grasp of the nature and mission of the church are intimately intertwined. It is only when we have grasped how the gospel gives birth to the church, and how the church witnesses (both by its proclamation and its life) to the gospel, that our witness to God's reconciling purpose for the world will achieve the clarity and power that God intends it to have.

3

COMMUNION

Dying and Rising with Jesus Christ

In the previous chapter, we underscored the importance of *participation* in the reign of God. We do not adequately understand the gospel if we think of it only as doctrinal content. Nor do we adequately understand the gospel if we think only of its benefits for us, or even its benefits for the world (e.g., forgiveness, justice, peace, reconciliation, etc.). We understand the gospel most clearly and most biblically when we think of receiving the gospel as participation in (that is, receiving, entering, proclaiming, and representing) the reign of God.

Christians believe that this new reality of God's reign has entered history not by human efforts, nor even by the general providence of God. Rather, the reign of God has entered history in the life, death, and resurrection of Jesus Christ. Jesus is the Messiah, the one anointed to reign in God's kingdom. It is through Jesus that God's generosity is extended most powerfully to the creation, and to Jesus that allegiance is to be returned. The most basic and earliest of all the Christian confessions is the acclamation, "Jesus is Lord." Therefore, we are far from finished with the matter when we insist that the reign of God must be understood in a participatory fashion. We must also inquire into the quality and character of the reign of God as it is revealed to us in Jesus of Nazareth.

In order for us to understand how the reign of God is revealed in Jesus, we need to cultivate a kind of stereoscopic vision. With one eye, we need to see Jesus as the anointed king, the Lord. He is the source of

God's grace, and the one to whom final allegiance is due. However, with the other eye, we need to see Jesus as the Son, the one who receives and trusts in God's generosity and maintains faithful allegiance to God when no one else does so. In other words, Jesus is presented to us in Scripture as both the model king and the model subject in the reign of God. With this stereoscopic view, the New Testament presents an integrated vision of what participating in God's life looks like, simply by referring to the life, death, and resurrection of Jesus. Jesus is both the Lord to be worshiped and the example to be imitated for those who wish to participate in God's reign.

But to speak of Jesus as an "example" does not quite convey, in our cultural context, the role that Jesus plays in the pages of the New Testament. In the ancient world, the character of the king determined the character of the nation that served him. Over and over in the Old Testament, the story of Israel is narrated with reference to the faithfulness of its kings to God. As the king went, so went the nation. So Jesus is presented in the New Testament not merely as a "role model" that one might, if one chose, try to imitate. Rather, Jesus is the King, and the quality and character of his life define the lives of those who give allegiance to him.

Perhaps a more contemporary analogy will be helpful here. When a new president is elected in the United States, he brings with him a new administration, composed of hundreds of governmental officials. These officials look to the president to discern how they are to conduct themselves. Not only the explicit policies of the president, but also the style, demeanor, and values of the president must shape the administration as a whole. The presidential transition in 2000 from Bill Clinton and his administration to the team of George W. Bush provided a dramatic example, as casually dressed, up-all-night, pizza-eating policy sessions in the White House gave way to a staff in suits who attended more formal meetings in a working day marked by a clear beginning and end.

This shift happens not just because it is the duty and responsibility of the administration to do the will of its president. It happens because the presidency is an institution of *power*. But the capacity of individuals in the administration to wield that power depends directly on the extent to which they are conformed to the model and example of the president. The whole administration acquires its identity through the behavior, values, and pronouncements of its president. In the same way, the early church looked to Jesus as the one who defined for them what life in the kingdom of God was like, and how it was to be lived. To the extent that the church was conformed to Christ, it also experienced the power of Christ in its life and witness.

But what a strange model Jesus was! He refused to use any military power, even shied away from having people call him the Messiah. He told his followers that if they wanted to be his disciples, they had to take up their crosses and follow him (Matt. 16:24; Mark 8:34; Luke 9:23). The early church took this saying very seriously. In fact, the most important way in which the early church thought Jesus should be imitated was in his death and resurrection. For the early Christians, death and resurrection marked the basic pattern that shaped life in the reign of God. The most important thing they saw in Jesus was his death and resurrection; his preaching, teaching, and healing ministry was understood in each of the gospels primarily to set the stage for these climactic events. To belong to Christ meant, therefore, that one somehow shared in his death and resurrection.

This communion with Christ in his death and resurrection is the central reality attested to by the sacraments of baptism and the Lord's Supper. Paul says in Romans 6:4, "Therefore we have been buried with him by baptism into death, so that, just as Christ was raised from the dead by the glory of the Father, so we too might walk in newness of life." Paul speaks of the bread and the cup as a "sharing" (*koinonia*, or "communion") in the body of Christ (1 Cor. 10:16). In Mark, Jesus speaks of his death as a "baptism" that others might receive as well (Mark 10:38-39). Clearly participating in God's reign is not merely akin to joining a religious organization. It involves communion in the divine life — a communion that is shaped and marked by Christ's death and resurrection.

The Work of the Holy Spirit

This chapter will explore more deeply what it means to say that belonging to Christ involves a communion with Christ, a sharing in his death and resurrection. In so doing, we will delve more deeply into what it means to participate in the reign of God. But first we need to look at the work of the Holy Spirit. We need to explore this topic because Scripture repeatedly draws a close connection between hearing the gospel (and participating in God's reign) and receiving the Holy Spirit. At Pentecost, the coming of the Spirit is directly associated with "speaking about God's deeds of power" (Acts 2:11). In Acts 10, as Peter proclaims the gospel to Cornelius and his household, "the Holy Spirit fell upon all who heard the word" (Acts 10:44). Paul's letters carry the same emphasis. When Paul speaks of the conversion of the Thessalonians, he speaks of how the "message of the gospel came to [them] not in word only, but also in power and in the Holy Spirit and with full conviction" (1 Thess. 1:5). Ephesians 1:13 links the gospel and the Spirit similarly: "In him you also, when you had heard the word of truth, the gospel of your salvation, and had believed in him, were marked with the seal of the promised Holy Spirit."

Clearly, receiving the gospel (in the full sense of participation in the reign of God) and receiving the Holy Spirit are directly linked in Scripture. Two additional scriptural themes expand upon this link between the Spirit and the gospel: The Holy Spirit is given to all believers, and the Spirit is given in the name of Jesus.

The Acts of the Apostles goes out of its way to emphasize that *everyone* who hears and fully believes in the gospel receives the Holy Spirit. The Pentecost event itself is presented as the fulfillment of the prophecy of Joel, "I will pour out my Spirit upon *all* flesh" (Acts 2:17, emphasis added). Repeatedly, the New Testament emphasizes that all Christians are recipients of the Spirit (e.g., Acts 10:44; Rom. 8:14; 1 Cor. 12:3, 13). The emphasis that the Spirit is given to all carries with it two important corollaries: First, there are no privileged few who have greater access to God than others — no priestly class, no clerical elite. The reign of God is not mediated to the masses through a few; it is rather a form of life in which all participate equally, a transformative power that is available to all without distinction or discrimination. Secondly, the Spirit is given *to the entire community* and not merely to individuals. Or to put it differently, the Spirit empowers a shared, communal form of life, in which individuals participate. The Spirit is not my personal means to holiness; the Spirit is rather the agent through whom a shared form of life comes into being.

The book of Acts also repeatedly emphasizes that the Spirit is given *in the name of Jesus*. The Spirit is directly connected to the person of Jesus. This emphasis receives further exposition in the Gospel according to John. Jesus declares, "I have said these things to you while I am still with you. But the Advocate, the Holy Spirit, whom the Father will send in my name, will teach you everything, and remind you of all that I have said to you" (John 14:25-26). Later, Jesus says that the Spirit "will glorify me, because he will take what is mine and declare it to you" (John 16:14). The emphasis in both these passages is that the Spirit maintains the personal presence of Jesus among the disciples, after Jesus' departure.

This emphasis is in keeping with the broader understanding of spirit in the ancient world, an understanding that is foreign to us in our modern culture. In the ancient world generally, spirit was the word used to describe the capacity for interpersonal knowing. Luke Johnson writes, "The power within humans to reach beyond their physical frames into the minds and hearts of others through knowledge and love is a pale intimation of what 'Holy Spirit' means when used of God, whose transcendence is marked by the capacity to be interior to all existence simultaneously, and present to all that is created without ever being defined by creation, without ever ceasing to be Other to all the sensible round of being."[1]

When Jesus says in John 16:14 that the Spirit will "take what is mine, and declare it to you," this is not merely a reference to imparting information. Rather, the Spirit mediates the quality and character of Jesus' life to the Christian community. Dying with Jesus and rising with Jesus become experienced realities in the Christian community through the work of the Holy Spirit. Thus, the frequent biblical call to imitate Christ is not given to isolated individuals trying to live like Jesus. It is rather an invitation to participate in the work of the Spirit, as the Spirit replicates the experience of Jesus among the people of God.

With that understanding, we can now turn to exploring the nature and character of Jesus' experience that is mediated to us by the Spirit. What does it mean to die and rise with Christ?

---

1. Johnson, *Living Jesus: Learning the Heart of the Gospel* (San Francisco: Harper-SanFrancisco, 1998), p. 16.

COMMUNION

Dying with Christ

North American Christians readily understand that Christ died for us, as a sacrifice for our sins. We are far less likely to understand the Bible's insistence that Christians are to be united with Christ in his death. Jesus declares in Mark 8:34-35, "If any want to become my followers, let them deny themselves and take up their cross and follow me. For those who want to save their life will lose it, and those who lose their life for my sake, and for the sake of the gospel, will save it" (cf. Matt. 16:24-28; Luke 9:23-27). Jesus' demand that his followers "eat his flesh and drink his blood" in John 6, cryptic as it may be, is probably a call to some kind of participation in Christ's death. Paul declares in Romans 6:5 that "we have been united with [Christ] in a death like his" and speaks of Christian life in general as "always carrying in the body the death of Jesus, so that the life of Jesus may also be made visible in our bodies" (2 Cor. 4:10). The first letter of Peter also speaks of our union with Christ in his sufferings: "Beloved, do not be surprised at the fiery ordeal that is taking place among you to test you, as though something strange were happening to you. But rejoice insofar as you are sharing Christ's sufferings, so that you may also be glad and shout for joy when his glory is revealed" (1 Pet. 4:12-13).

North American Christians tend to prefer a religion of receiving to a religion of participation. It is not coincidence, then, that North American Christians are clearer on the sacrifice of Christ *for us* than they are on our *participation* in the sacrifice of Christ. And yet, the Bible speaks as if Christ's death *for us* merely provides the possibility of our participation in his death. To be sure, Christ's death accomplishes our forgiveness and reconciliation to God. This is the joyous and wonderful beginning to the good news. We are freed from our sins and given a new start. We can leave behind our shameful pasts and be forgiven of all our failures, weaknesses, and shortcomings. Thanks be to God! But this is only the beginning of the good news. We are forgiven and reconciled so that we can participate in Christ's mission to the world, a mission marked by death and resurrection as its fundamental pattern.

But what does it mean for Christians to participate in Christ's death? This is a huge topic that can be explored from many vantage points. The one that may be most helpful for us is the social context of the ancient world. From that viewpoint, we can begin to understand what being crucified with Christ is all about.

For the message about the cross is foolishness to those who are perishing, but to us who are being saved it is the power of God. For it is written,

"I will destroy the wisdom of the wise,
and the discernment of the discerning I will thwart."

Where is the one who is wise? Where is the scribe? Where is the debater of this age? Has not God made foolish the wisdom of the world? For since, in the wisdom of God, the world did not know God through wisdom, God decided, through the foolishness of our proclamation, to save those who believe. For Jews demand signs and Greeks desire wisdom, but we proclaim Christ crucified, a stumbling block to Jews and foolishness to Gentiles, but to those who are the called, both Jews and Greeks, Christ the power of God and the wisdom of God. For God's foolishness is wiser than human wisdom, and God's weakness is stronger than human strength.

1 Corinthians 1:18-25

The cross has become the central symbol of Christian faith, but for many of us today, it is so commonplace that it no longer sparks our imaginations. It easily becomes an empty symbol, something to put at the front of churches, something to make necklaces out of, to add to a charm bracelet, or something to reflect on in theological abstraction. That was not at all the case when Paul was writing his letters. Then, the cross represented the most brutal kind of death by torture. It was not a source of comfort to people; the cross was not a religious symbol of any sort prior to Christianity. When Paul speaks of the foolishness of the cross, he is talking about the offensiveness of bringing something so ugly to the center of faith.

To talk about a cross in the ancient world would be like talking today about instruments of torture. Listen to some of the ways people in the ancient world talked about crucifixion: "Punished with limbs out-stretched, they see the stake as their fate; they are fastened and nailed to it in the most bitter torment, evil food for birds of prey and grim pickings for dogs."[2]

Often by the time someone came to take the bodies down from crosses, birds and wild animals had not left much to be taken. The Roman poet Juvenal writes, "The vulture hurries from dead cattle and dogs and crosses to bring some of the carrion to her offspring."

Another Roman writer, Seneca, speaks of the variety of creative options open to the sadistic executioner: "I see crosses there, not just of one kind but made in many different ways: some have their victims with head down to the ground; some impale their private parts; others stretch out their arms on the gibbet."

Sometimes people would be nailed to crosses; at other times, they were simply impaled on stakes. Crucifixion was almost always preceded by some other form of torture that gave the executioner an opportunity to display his virtuosity. Jesus was flogged. Others would have their eyes gouged out, or their tongues cut out, or have limbs broken.

We don't include this information to titillate or offend, nor do we mention these things to try to magnify appreciation for the death of Jesus in particular, important as that may be. Instead, we believe it is important to evoke something of what it must have been like in the ancient world to hear talk about crucifixion. We need to gain some grasp of what people in Paul's day would have thought and felt when they heard the word "cross." It wasn't pretty. It wasn't nice. And once that reality is clearly in our minds, we are ready to understand the social implications of worshiping someone who was crucified.

Crucifixion was not the general form of capital punishment in the Roman Empire of Jesus' day; it was rarely done to Roman citizens. It was reserved instead for particular classes of people: people who committed especially violent or repugnant crimes, people who engaged in sedition against the Roman government, and slaves who rebelled against their masters. In other words, crucifixion was essentially a device used by the

---

2. This translation is drawn from the translations in Martin Hengel's helpful book, *Crucifixion in the Ancient World and the Folly of the Message of the Cross* (Philadelphia: Fortress Press, 1977), p. 9. The reader of Hengel's monograph will easily discern the ways in which his research illumines many points in this chapter.

Romans to terrorize potentially dangerous populations into submission. It was used against those groups who posed the greatest threat to the security of society, and it was designed — intentionally — to be so horrifying and gruesome that these groups would not dare to act against the establishment. That's why the executioner was to display all his virtuosity in making the death as miserable and offensive as possible.

Consequently, many people in the ancient world would have had a kind of instinctive revulsion to anyone who had been crucified. To be crucified meant to be in the class of subversives, the worst of criminals, and rebellious slaves — in other words, to be at the bottom of the societal heap, to be a danger to society. You get a feel for what it was like to talk about someone who was crucified by this quote from Cicero:

> How grievous a thing it is to be disgraced by a public court; how grievous to suffer a fine, how grievous to suffer banishment; and yet in the midst of any such disaster we retain some degree of liberty. Even if we are threatened with death, we may die free men. But the executioner, the veiling of the head and the very word "cross" should be far removed not only from the person of a Roman citizen but from his thoughts, his eyes, and his ears. For it is not only the actual occurrence of these things or the endurance of them, but liability to them, the expectation, indeed the very mention of them, that is unworthy of a Roman citizen and a free man.[3]

So the crucifixion was an emotionally shocking, even a shattering event for early believers. It has also represented a real problem in missionary preaching, because as a missionary you may not even get a hearing after saying that Jesus was crucified. You might even be suspected of being a subversive yourself.

What is especially striking about the early church, however, is that it made no attempt to diminish the offensiveness of its message by downplaying the crucifixion. One could imagine a quiet sweeping under the rug of the details and circumstances of Jesus' death. In fact, precisely this happened in a story of a Roman general, Regulus, who was captured and crucified by the enemies of Rome and became a kind of national martyr. Only the earliest accounts of his life mention the fact

---

3. Cicero, *Pro Rabirio*, ch. 16, trans. Hengel in *Crucifixion*, p. 42.

that he had been crucified. In later, more developed accounts of his death, there is no mention of the fact that he was crucified.[4]

Christianity, by contrast, focused upon and preoccupied itself with this offense. Rather than accommodating themselves to normal human tastes and sensibilities, early Christian preachers threw this offense into the face of the world. Madison Avenue would never have counseled such a move: too many negatives to make the cross so central. But there it is, at the center of Paul's discourse.

And the question, of course, is why? Why couldn't the early church have just said that Christ died for our sins, without talking about how he died? We come at this point to the very center of Christian faith, and we could probably give dozens of answers to the question of why the cross of Jesus is so central. But let us offer at least a few possible answers.

First, and perhaps most importantly, the message of the cross means that the church is, in very fundamental ways, a community that radically calls into question the status quo. Any group that worships a crucified person will have difficulty functioning as the Chamber of Commerce. Any community of people that celebrates the fact that God redeems the world through a crucified Messiah will also be a community that celebrates how God continues to work in unexpected, unconventional, and unpredictable ways. The message of the cross invites us to look to a God who works from the bottom up and from the margins inward, rather than from the top down. Christianity has not often functioned with spiritual vitality in the mainstream of a culture. There's something about that location which often seems to blunt the energizing and disruptive power of the cross.

This does not mean that the gospel must always spawn a sectarian and separatist life in order to have integrity. It's rather the case that the message of the cross jars Christians loose from normal assumptions and expectations. It gives them an odd, quirky way of looking at the world, in whatever social location they may find themselves.

Not only does the cross create a kind of dislocation with respect to the dominant society, but the apocalyptic storm front of God's engagement with the creation is echoed within us as well. The cross creates an internal dislocation and turbulence. It cuts across our normal hopes, dreams, and expectations for our own lives. It suggests that God's work

4. See the discussion in Hengel, *Crucifixion*, pp. 64ff.

in our lives emerges in the most surprising and unexpected ways: in the brokenness, the darkness, the loneliness of our lives.

But there's more to the gospel than just oddness. This is not a romantic vision of walking to the beat of a different drummer. The cross is not merely countercultural, not merely a critical and negative principle; it has its own constructive message as well. In the midst of all its disturbing offensiveness and strangeness, the cross speaks powerfully of radical love and radical trust. It shows just how far God is willing to go to show his love to us, in the life of Jesus who gives up his life for his friends. And it shows just how far humanity can go in trusting obedience to God in the life of Jesus, who trustingly obeys God's will, even when it costs him his life. The cross shatters our conventional understandings of what it means to love, of what propriety and decorum are all about. It breaks the boundaries that enclose how far we think God can be trusted. And it calls us to a profoundly different kind of life: loving, trusting, and risking more deeply than we otherwise would have thought possible.

Perhaps all this feels a little overwhelming. Most of us will confess to such feelings. Every time we hear the Beatitudes, something in us gets uncomfortable. We wonder what we will have to give up, what we will lose, what unhappiness we must endure if we are to follow Jesus Christ. But it is at precisely that point, when our defenses start to rise, that we need to hear again about the promise and help of the Holy Spirit.

We need to hear about the Spirit, because one of the most important things the Bible has to say about the Spirit is that the Spirit has many ways to form Jesus Christ in us. Paul's image for the work of the Spirit is the body, where differentiation is what enables the body to function at all. There is not just one way to live a life under the sign of the cross. The Spirit inspires many ways. A look at the early church gives some ideas. The early church found a variety of ways to express the "no" to human assumptions and values that is implicit in the cross. Some early Christians lived lives of radical voluntary poverty. A good example is found in Jesus' commission to his own disciples before their preaching tour in Matthew 10:5-10 and Luke 10:1-12. Here they are to take no money, not even a spare set of clothes. They are to be living examples of a radical trust in God, a kind of trust that shatters our ordinary assumptions about what we "need to get by." They are to be a living sign that shakes the world loose from its anxious reliance upon possessions. In this sense, they are a precursor to the cross itself.

But notice something. Who takes care of these itinerant poor preachers? Believers! Those who had homes, families, and food to spare! Without them, the preaching missions would have been impossible. Hence this call to radical poverty is not a call to the whole church, but it is a call to some in the church as an expression of the cross.

Likewise Paul calls some to celibacy in 1 Corinthians 7:32-35. These people are a sign to the world that sex is not the be-all and end-all of life. But again, this call is not for everyone.

The Christians in Acts 4 shared their possessions as a radical challenge to the world's tendency to horde and isolate. But again, there is no evidence that this pattern was normative in early Christianity generally.

That diversity is scattered throughout the pages of the New Testament. Some Christians gave up their lives in martyrdom. Others opened wide the doors of their houses in hospitality to whole congregations. They poured themselves out in concern for the poor; they experimented with whole new patterns of relating to each other — patterns that cut against the static hierarchies of the day. In countless ways, both great and small, they challenged with their lives the prevailing assumptions of the day, and like a prism they refracted the light of God's grace into many colors.

We believe that the church today needs to be both as radical and as diverse as it was in those early days — as it has always been at its best. At its best, the church has affirmed those who are called to a radical simplicity of lifestyle, to remind the rest of us that we don't need what we think we need. The church has understood the value of people committed to celibacy, who remind us that sex is neither a necessity nor a god. We have learned from those who continually open their homes to others, who cure the rest of us of the idolatry of our privacy. We are nourished by devoted parents who sacrifice career advancement for the sake of time with their children, who help the rest of us keep our priorities straight. We are strengthened by people who are lavish in prayer and spiritual disciplines, who remind those of us with harder spirits of where our real help comes from and goad us out of our complacency. The church thrives when it is made up of communities of Christians willing to commit themselves to support each other in risky, venturesome ways, when Christians are willing to resist creatively the many ways in which the dominant in our world crush the weak.

In short, the gospel resounds in the life of the church when Christians find a thousand joyful ways to take the mixed-up values of this world and turn them upside down — when Christians aren't afraid to walk down a path the world calls madness, a path that is really the road to life. In this each of us will have a distinctive calling. But that calling is discerned and embraced within the context of a loving and discerning community. It is vitally important that we not carry someone else's cross, but rather that our eyes are fixed firmly on where Jesus is calling us. But it is also vital for us to encourage each other in our shared discipleship. In this way, each individual life bears witness to the power of the cross, and the shared life of the entire community bears witness with harmony, unity, and power to the mysterious way in which God brings life out of what the world calls death. Then, and only then, will we discover the resolution to one of the greatest paradoxes in all of Scripture: on the one hand, we are all to take up our crosses daily; on the other hand, what Jesus says is absolutely true — "my yoke is easy, and my burden is light" (Matt. 11:30). This is what it means to participate in the reign of God and to be united with Christ in his death. This is the life that the gospel invites Christians to receive, to enter, and to proclaim.

Rising with Christ

But there is more to the gospel than dying with Christ. The gospel comes to its climax in the announcement that Christ has been raised from the dead and has ascended to heaven, "far above all rule and authority and power and dominion, and above every name that is named, not only in this age but also in the age to come" (Eph. 1:21). The letter to the Ephesians goes on to point out that Christ has accomplished this "for the church, which is his body" (1:22-23). For many North American Christians, the resurrection of Jesus functions primarily as an assurance of their own life after death, as well as an assurance that they will see their deceased loved ones again. While we affirm and celebrate such assurances, this perspective scarcely does adequate justice to all that the Bible has to say about Jesus' resurrection. In particular, this perspective says little about what it might mean to think about the meaning of our participation in Christ's resurrection here and now.

North American Christians find it hard to grasp participating in Christ's resurrection in part because we are so removed from the cul-

> God put this power to work in Christ when he raised him
> from the dead and seated him at his right hand in the heav-
> enly places, far above all rule and authority and power and
> dominion, and above every name that is named, not only in
> this age but also in the age to come. And he has put all things
> under his feet and has made him the head over all things for
> the church, which is his body, the fullness of him who fills all
> in all.
>
> Ephesians 1:20-23

tural context of the Bible. In order to grasp fully the meaning and significance of Christ's resurrection, it will help first to go back to the Old
Testament. Most of the Old Testament has very little to say about resurrection at all. In most of the Old Testament, the mark of God's blessing is to live a long and full life and then to die and rest with the ancestors. Salvation in the Old Testament is almost entirely focused upon
this world. Dying of old age does not break off the life that is blessed by
God but is its natural completion.

For much of the Old Testament, this focus upon the present life is
accompanied by an urgent summons to obedience and faithfulness.
The end of the book of Deuteronomy summarizes the perspective well:

> See, I have set before you today life and prosperity, death and ad-
> versity. If you obey the commandments of the Lord your God that
> I am commanding you today, by loving the Lord your God, walk-
> ing in his ways, and observing his commandments, decrees, and
> ordinances, then you shall live and become numerous, and the
> Lord your God will bless you in the land that you are entering to
> possess. But if your heart turns away and you do not hear, but are
> led astray to bow down to other gods and serve them, I declare to
> you today that you shall perish; you shall not live long in the land
> that you are crossing the Jordan to enter and possess (30:15-18).

Obedience brings life and blessing; disobedience and faithlessness
bring death, destruction, sickness, and calamity. Over and over, through-

out the Bible's narration of Israel's history, these realities appear and re-appear. Israel is faithful and experiences God's blessing; Israel is disobedient and comes under God's judgment, finally ending in exile.

In the period after Israel's exile, however, this understanding of the relationship between life and obedience came under severe testing. In the second century BCE, the people of God came under the domination of a cruel tyrant, Antiochus Epiphanes, who declared Judaism to be an illegal religion and threatened those who practiced it with death. (The apocryphal books of Maccabees narrate the story.) Antiochus precipitated a cruel inversion of the book of Deuteronomy. He put those who were faithful to God's law to death and allowed those who disobeyed the law to live.

It was during this period that the first Old Testament books were written that speak explicitly and at length of the resurrection of the righteous (e.g., Daniel 11:35; 12:2, etc.).[5] The logic that drives these books appears to operate in this fashion: If God is faithful, just, and the ruler over the whole earth (and these are attributes of God that cannot in any way be doubted), and if God's faithfulness, justice, and sovereignty do not fully appear in this life, then there must be a life after death in which God's faithfulness, justice, and sovereignty will be manifest.

This emergence of explicit discussion of resurrection appears alongside another new literary form in this period: apocalyptic literature. Apocalyptic literature develops and systematizes a distinction between "this age," marked by suffering and injustice, and "the age to come," in which God's righteousness and faithfulness will be fully known and experienced. In these texts, the discussion of the resurrection of the just goes hand in hand with a discussion of the "age to come." The age to come is both the time of resurrection and the time for the final and thorough establishment of God's justice.

Clear talk about resurrection in the Old Testament, then, is characterized by two important themes connected with God's justice. First, resurrection is intimately tied to the vindication of the righteous; and, second, resurrection is also intimately tied to the coming age, when God's sovereignty and righteousness will be universally manifested, and when God's faithfulness will be unquestionable.

---

5. 2 Maccabees 7:9, 11, 14.

The New Testament writers look at the resurrection of Jesus against this backdrop. The resurrection of Jesus vindicates him as Messiah and confirms his message, in the face of his humiliating death (e.g., Acts 4:10-11). But much more importantly, the resurrection of Jesus signals the onset of "the age to come," in which all of God's saving purposes for the world come to their culmination, and in which God establishes righteousness on earth. Paul's use of this apocalyptic framework is clear in one of the earliest New Testament passages, 1 Thessalonians 1:9-10: "For the people of those regions report about us what kind of welcome we had among you, and how you turned to God from idols, to serve a living and true God, and to wait for his Son from heaven, whom he raised from the dead — Jesus, who rescues us from the wrath that is coming." Notice how closely in Paul's mind the resurrection of Jesus is associated with the coming wrath, when God's sovereign justice and righteousness will be made fully known.

At the same time, we find in the New Testament something that is completely unprecedented in Jewish sources before Christianity: the notion that the resurrection of the Messiah precedes the general resurrection. This new development results in one of the most important features of the New Testament: the tension between the "already" and the "not yet." On the one hand, the resurrection of Jesus suggests that the new age has come, a theme that is repeated at many points in the New Testament (e.g., John 11:25). On the other hand, the ongoing reality of death and suffering indicates that the age to come has not fully arrived (e.g., Rom. 8:19-25). The New Testament portrays all of Christian life in the midst of this tension.

This brief survey of biblical backgrounds makes it clear that the Bible's discussion of the resurrection of Jesus is not primarily concerned with the human quest for immortality. The biblical background suggests that the central issues at stake have to do with God's justice, faithfulness, and sovereignty. The resurrection is all about whether God can be trusted, even though God's faithfulness and justice may not always appear in this life, and God's sovereignty may seem utterly absent. When the gospel declares that God raised Jesus from the dead, it affirms that God is faithful to all the covenant promises, and that nothing — not even death — can stand in the way of God's justice and faithfulness. The gospel declares that the resurrection of Jesus is a sure ground for hope, even though all the evidences of God's righteousness and faithfulness may not present themselves in our experience yet. We know that death is defeated, and that God's faithfulness is sure.

But what does it mean to *participate* in the resurrection of Jesus? How does the gospel invite us and make it possible for us to enact, or *perform,* this story in the life of the new people of God, the church? We would suggest three ways in which the church is called to participate in Christ's resurrection. First, the church is the community of God's people that knows that nothing can separate us from the love and faithfulness of God, and lives in the light of this knowledge. Second, the church is the community of God's people that knows that death is defeated, and lives in the light of this knowledge. Third, the church is the community of God's people that knows that the powers of the universe are subject to Christ, and lives in the light of this knowledge. As we shall see, these three aspects of participating in Christ's resurrection are closely interrelated.

Living in God's Faithfulness

We live in a society that is undergoing massive changes. Many of these changes focus on the accelerating pace of change. Businesses reinvent themselves almost annually. Many communities are going through rapid transitions, some for the better, some for the worse. Personal relationships also move on a fast track. This accelerating pace of change also exacts a toll upon us. In the United States, one-half of all marriages will end in divorce. The gap between rich and poor is widening, and though many are finding a way out of poverty, the remaining poor seem more entrenched than ever. In many other parts of the world, accelerating change means improving standards of living and technological development, but also accelerating depletion of natural resources, disruption of traditional forms of life, urbanization, pollution, AIDS, and crime. The accelerating pace of change in our society tends to force people even more powerfully into individualism. When everything is changing all around you, you need to watch out first of all for yourself. Loyalty and allegiance appear more naïve than virtuous. Short-term, utilitarian relationships become the norm.

The church that lives by the gospel is called by that gospel to a different kind of life. The church is called to model a form of life in which faithfulness, love, and allegiance are not merely utilitarian virtues to be discarded when inconvenient, but rather the bedrock upon which life is built. Participating in resurrection life means living as if love really is stronger than death, as if faithfulness really is more powerful than the naked pursuit of self-interest. In the midst of a society that believes that all bets must be hedged, that all loyalties must be conditioned upon self-interest, the church dares to live differently.

One sees this clearly in texts such as Colossians 3. Paul begins by affirming that we have been raised with Christ. He then goes on to reason from this reality to a wide range of practical consequences for the way in which people relate to each other: "But now you must get rid of all such things — anger, wrath, malice, slander, and abusive language from your mouth. Do not lie to one another, seeing that you have been stripped of the old self with its practices and have clothed yourselves with the new self, which is being renewed in knowledge according to the image of its creator" (Col. 3:8-10).

This difference is based upon the life and example of Jesus. It is a life marked by the making and keeping of promises and commitments. It is a life nourished by committed long-term relationships dedicated to the common good — in marriage, in Christian fellowships, in neighborhoods. It is a life predicated upon the assumption that people change and grow best in committed, long-term relationships, rather than in constantly changing patterns of connection to others. It is a form of life that deeply challenges the prevailing social assumption that self-interest is the most inviolable feature of every social interaction.

Of course, such a form of life is rarely easy. Jesus' commitment to his friends and to his mission cost him his life. But the church nourished by the gospel hope of resurrection knows that such apparent failures or setbacks cannot make the slightest dent in the fundamental power of God's love, expressed in faithfulness and loyalty.

Living as if Death Is Defeated

It is no small thing to claim that death is defeated. Of course, our culture claims, in hundreds of small ways, to defeat death every day. If we purchase the right cosmetics, eat the right foods, follow the right diet, eat the right supplements, live the right lifestyle — then we will surely live forever, or at least death will be held at bay. We live in a society that devotes enormous amounts of time and energy to denying or attempting to elude the grip of death. Health care is one of the most rapidly expanding sectors of our economy. Death takes place only in specialized locations, far from the normal buzz of life.

But it is not only our relentless pursuit of health that is driven by the fear of death. Ernest Becker, in his seminal study *The Denial of Death,* points out how the pursuit of the heroic, so dominant in Western culture, is essentially an attempt to elude the power of death, an attempt somehow to achieve significance as a person in the face of the relentless leveling and forgetfulness of death.[6] Andy Warhol's famous quip that everyone will have his (or her) fifteen minutes of fame underscores ironically the self-defeating way in which the thirst for significance becomes trivial precisely by its pervasiveness in the culture. Humans can never defeat or elude death. Our ceaseless attempts to do so are always haunted by the prospect of their inevitable failure. Analysts such as Freud have discerned the extent to which even many Christian attempts to claim the defeat of death appear, on closer analysis, to be exercises in wish fulfillment and illusion, subtle masks for our own dreams of omnipotence and our narcissistic self-absorption.

The letter to the Hebrews is correct, therefore, when it speaks of how people "all their lives were held in slavery by the fear of death" (Heb. 2:15). The fear of death enslaves not only through the threat of despair, but even more powerfully through our insatiable thirst for significance and our relentless drive for the heroic. To accept ourselves as "merely ordinary" is to acknowledge that death is the great leveler, and we are loath to do this, even though something deep within us knows it to be true.

So what does it mean to participate in Christ's resurrection and to live in the knowledge of death's defeat? It means, first of all, to accept one's ordinariness, to let go of our endless and futile attempts to make ourselves significant or extraordinary. This does not mean that we sink into a mass of bland humanity. It means that we simply accept life as God's gift, precious in itself, not because of our efforts, but because of God's generosity. To live in the knowledge of death's defeat is therefore

6. Becker *The Denial of Death* (New York: The Free Press, 1973).

the very opposite of Freud's notion of resurrection as wish fulfillment. Rather, it is precisely in the ruthless identification of our own illusory dreams and the relinquishing of the efforts driven by those fantasies that we can receive life as a gift that is validated and made secure, not by our own efforts, but by the mercy of the God who is the author of life.

Confronting the Powers

The fear of death is not only a problem for individuals, however. It is also a powerful force — perhaps the most powerful force — in society as a whole. Most of the efforts of civilizations throughout history have been devoted to staving off the power of death. This happens directly through the pursuit of health, stable agricultural production, peace, and security. But it also happens metaphorically, as cultures devote enormous amounts of energy to constructing architectural, artistic, cultural, and intellectual "monuments" that will withstand the ravages of time and decay.

There is nothing inherently wrong with efforts to prolong, sustain, and enhance life. However, when such collective efforts are driven by the fear of death, they can easily claim absolute allegiance and become destructive. This is, in essence, the phenomenon that the Bible describes using the language of "principalities and powers." A careful look at some biblical background can help us understand this phenomenon.

It is important to recognize first of all that the Bible uses a fluid and somewhat interchangeable set of words to describe powers that are at work in governments and other collective expressions of human life. The vocabulary includes words such as *archon* (ruler), *exousiai* (authorities), *dunamai* (powers), *kuriotes* (dominion), but it is not always clear when these are referring to human rulers, and when to forces that transcend people. Passages such as Luke 12:11, Romans 13:1-2, and Titus 3:1 all seem to refer to earthly rulers, whereas other texts such as Ephesians 6:12 and 1 Peter 3:22 use the same words in ways that clearly refer to some sort of transcendent powers.

This ambiguity between earthly and transcendent powers goes back to Old Testament roots. In a variety of passages, an angelic figure is described, but in a way that is very closely connected with a particular government or other human collectivity (e.g., Deut. 32:8-9; Ps. 82:1-4; Dan. 10:13-14). This ambiguity suggests that the Bible has a clear sense that human collective activity is greater than the sum of its parts and acquires its own quasi-independent existence. Whether these "powers" are personal beings, or "only" impersonal social forces need not detain us at this point. Suffice it to observe that the Bible speaks of transcendent spiritual forces that are closely linked with human collectivities.

A glance at some other New Testament passages fills out this picture. We first observe that these powers are created by God, for the purpose of serving and praising God. Colossians 1:16 states, "In [Christ] all things in heaven and on earth were created, things visible and invisible, whether thrones or dominions or rulers or powers — all things have been created through him and for him." The capacity of human beings to form collectivities that exceed the sum of their parts is a capacity given by God in creation.

These powers are intimately related to human *systems* and *structures* (hence the ambiguity between human rulers and transcendent powers). Today we speak of the "spirit of an organization." The Bible would speak of the "angel" or "principality" of an organization (cf. the "angels" of the seven churches in Revelation). Collectivities have lives of their own, independent of the individuals involved. Yet these powers share in the fallenness of creation. As fallen entities, they often resist God and enslave human beings. Evil is not only personal; it has a transcendent dimension. For this reason, the New Testament can speak of salvation as deliverance from the powers (e.g., Col. 2:13-15; Eph. 2:1-2; Rom. 8:38-39). In this light, it should also be observed that, while the New Testament seems to indicate that some of the powers are destined only for destruction (e.g., 1 Cor. 15:24-26), others seem destined for redemption (Col. 1:16-19)

What is most striking about the New Testament's treatment of the powers, however, is that deliverance from the powers is usually associated in the New Testament with Christ's resurrection and ascension (Eph. 1:20-21; Col. 2:13-15; 1 Pet. 3:22). In other words, the defeat of death and the subjugation of hostile powers are conceived as parts of the same reality, part of the broad gospel exposition of the resurrection of Jesus. The New Testament seems to regard death as the greatest of all the powers, the central power from which every other fallen power draws its strength. Paul speaks of death reigning in Romans 5:14 and goes on to affirm that death no longer has dominion over Christ (Rom. 6:9). Consequently, in Paul's great affirmation of Christian security and confidence, he declares first that neither death nor life will be able to separate believers from the love of God and then immediately goes on to insist that the same applies to "angels," "rulers," and "powers" (Rom. 8:38-39).

The notion of death as the central power underlying all the other errant powers is even clearer in 1 Corinthians 15:24-26: "Then comes the end, when he hands over the kingdom to God the Father, after he has destroyed every ruler and every authority and power. For he must reign until he has put all his enemies under his feet. The last enemy to be destroyed is death."

This link between death and the principalities and powers gives us a clue as to how we are called to participate in Christ's resurrection. The New Testament suggests that all the principalities and powers that impinge on human life are fallen, insofar as they are dominated by the power of death. Death is the "last enemy." But what is the power of death, and how does it dominate human collectivities and systems?

The answer to that question becomes clearer once it is seen that the Bible regards the powers as being in rebellion against God. Because the powers, and the collective human efforts they represent, are alienated from the life-giving God, they claim their own existence as the absolute, highest good. In this sense, they are dominated by the fear of death. Apart from God, all human efforts are dominated first and foremost by the need for self-preservation at all costs. Civilizations, corporations, groups, and institutions are inherently incapable of contemplating their own demise with anything other than horror. Their self-preservation precedes all other responsibilities or allegiances. Yet this absolute claim to existence becomes powerfully idolatrous, as human collectivities demand for themselves absolute allegiance and place their own survival and flourishing ahead of the common good and God's purposes for creation as a whole. When organizations, governments, and associations of any sort become ends in themselves, losing sight of their call to praise God and serve God's purposes for creation as a whole, they become demonic and evil.

The gospel, however, offers a profoundly different vision, with its invitation to participate in resurrection life. Christians who participate in the good news know that death has been defeated. They know that institutional self-preservation is not the greatest of all goods. They are, in other words, freed from the corporate fear of death, set free to invite institutions, corporations, and other human collectivities to fulfill their God-given purposes. Christians model this in their own corporate life in the church and commend this liberating mode of corporate life to the world as a whole. Christians are those who know that it is only through the lordship of Christ, who has defeated death, that human beings are set free from their anxious obsession with preserving their own lives and set free to participate in all of God's purposes for creation as a whole.

What then does it mean to participate in the resurrection of Jesus? It means to live a life that is grounded in profound trust toward God, confident that God is faithful, just, loving, and the Lord of the universe. At the personal level, Christ's resurrection liberates us from the anxious thirst for significance, freeing us to receive God's life as a gift, entrusting ourselves to our faithful creator. Corporately, rising with Christ means that the power of death has been broken, the old idolatrous powers have been conquered, and governments and institutions are set free from the anxious compulsion to self-preservation and are invited to fulfill their purposes within God's intention for all of creation. Christians are those who see clearly these saving purposes that God has brought to light in the gospel, who model them in their own lives, and who commend them to the world by their words and deeds.

Conclusion

The centrality of our dying and rising with Christ is seen nowhere more clearly than in the sacraments. Paul explicitly connects baptism with our union with Christ in death and resurrection in Romans 6. In the Lord's Supper, we remember Jesus' death, share in his presence, and anticipate his coming again. To deepen our appropriation of the gospel is therefore at the same time to reappropriate the sacraments, the means by which God draws us into the divine life and shares that life with us.

The previous chapter suggested that we North Americans need to reconsider the gospel as an invitation to participate in God's mission to the world. In this chapter, we have explored what that participation looks like when lived out in the life of the church. Our exploration suggests that there is an intimate, organic connection between our participating in the gospel and our proclamation of the gospel. We can proclaim the gospel only insofar as we participate in the reality it announces, and our participation in the gospel is in itself a proclamation to the world of a new form of life in fellowship with God and with each other.

In this sense, the gospel is not just news to be heard. It is something like the script of a play to be performed. It is only when the world sees the radical love and radical trust lived out by those whose lives are transformed by the message of the cross that it will begin to hope that in this "foolishness" lies a deeper wisdom. It is only when the world sees a community freed from the fear of death and joyfully embracing its own vocation that it may catch a glimpse of the "new creation," the radically alternative form of human life announced by the gospel. It is only as the Spirit of God forms the reality of Jesus Christ within the church that the world may glimpse the truth that there are powers in this world greater than money, politics, and prestige.

That is why Jesus teaches that the church should be perfect, even as God is perfect (Matt. 5:48). Yet this perfection manifests itself not in the absence of creaturely flaws, weaknesses, or sins, but in the capacity of the church to be caught up into the depths of God's love. This love expresses itself most clearly in the church's love for its enemies and its radical forgiveness of others (Matt. 5:43-47). Though we continually fall short of this calling, it remains our divinely appointed destiny, towards which we pray and labor.

The church is always also the prime exhibit of God's grace, which is effective despite our failures and shortcomings. But this acknowledgment of human failure must never obscure the purpose for which the gospel itself is given: to announce to the world the new reality of the kingdom of God and to invite people to participate in that reality, despite their brokenness and shortcomings. The church must not allow its humble awareness of its failings to obscure its vision of the deeper reality of its union with Jesus Christ, who has embraced and conquered death, and who makes this power available to us in the Body of Christ through the Holy Spirit. This is good news — good news worth proclaiming to the world with our words and our lives!

4

POWERS

The Church and the Life of the World

In our last chapter we were bold to proclaim: "Rising with Christ means that the power of death has been broken, the old idolatrous powers have been conquered, and governments and institutions are set free from the anxious compulsion to self-preservation and are invited to fulfill their purposes within God's intention for all of creation." How, then, can we believe and live this way, in the world as we know it today? Are the powers of this age really subject to the crucified and risen Christ? Is it really true, as the Apostle Paul said, that the weak things of God are stronger than human strength (1 Cor. 1:25)? Can that really be true? Is the world really like that?

We long to believe in such a world. We celebrate it every year. For centuries Christmas — the coming of God into this world in the birth of a helpless child — has been a holiday more beloved, although not more important, than Easter. We love its simple paradox:

Child in the manger,
Infant of Mary,
Outcast and stranger,
Lord of all.

We wonder at its contrasts: the shepherds in the field and the angels singing in heaven, the baby born in a stable and the magi from the East who honored him, the weary travelers shut out from the inn and

77

the humble arrival of the Lord, the Savior of the world. We weave our yearnings around this wonderful story and give ourselves to it. Luther's words five centuries ago still echo in our hearts:

> See how God invites you in many ways. He places before you a Babe with whom you may take refuge. You cannot fear him, for nothing is more appealing to us than a babe. Are you affrighted? Then come to him, lying in the lap of the sweetest and fairest maid. You will see how great is the divine goodness, which seeks above all else that you should not despair, Trust him! Trust him! Here is the child in whom is salvation. To me there is no greater consolation given to humankind than this, that Christ became man, a child, a babe, playing in the lap and at the breasts of his most gracious mother. Who is there whom this sight would not comfort? Now is overcome the power of sin, death, hell, conscience and guilt, if you come to this gurgling babe and believe that he is come not to judge you, but to save.

To be sure we sentimentalize the story. We surround it with warm feelings, good food, and the enjoyment of family and friends. We materialize it with trees and gifts and decorations. We build a culture around it and almost bury it with our music and our celebration. For a while we see ourselves as good and loving people bathed, at least until January, in the Christmas spirit.

But still the story itself breaks through: the power and love of almighty God born a helpless child in a world ruled by the power of others, for the salvation of us all. For a few days we act as if, despite all else we know about ourselves and our world, this story were really true.

But God does not leave us at this point of easy faith. Look at the contrast between our celebration of Christmas and of Easter. Jesus has grown up. He has become a perverse nonconformist in relation to political power, economic power, and the whole self-assertive ethos of a culture. He is a prophet with no status except his message. He has taken the form of a servant. The reign of God that he proclaims, as he made clear to Pilate, is not one of the powers of this world. He is disgraced and crucified. And, in the ultimate worldly put-down, "The

---

1. R. F. Bainton, ed., *The Martin Luther Christmas Book* (Philadelphia: Muhlenberg Press, 1959), p. 40.

> He is the image of the invisible God, the firstborn of all creation; for in him all things in heaven and on earth were created, things visible and invisible, whether thrones or dominions or rulers or powers — all things have been created through him and for him. He himself is before all things, and in him all things hold together. He is the head of the body, the church; he is the beginning, the firstborn from the dead, so that he might come to have first place in everything. For in him all the fullness of God was pleased to dwell, and through him God was pleased to reconcile to himself all things, whether on earth or in heaven, by making peace through the blood of his cross.
>
> Colossians 1:15-20

leaders scoffed at him, saying, 'He saved others; let him save himself if he is the Messiah of God, his chosen one'" (Luke 23:35).

This is the man who, we are asked to believe, rose from the dead to be Lord and Christ, in whom and through whom, as the letter to the Colossians declares, all the "thrones or dominions or rulers or powers" were created and hold together (1:16-17). This is the one whose reign, the final pages of the New Testament say, will be fulfilled in a new heaven and a new earth, a holy city come down from heaven in which "the home of God is among mortals. He will dwell with them as their God; they will be his peoples, and God himself will be with them" (Rev. 21:3).

We confess that victory, that hope. It is our gospel — the good news we have to offer the world. The church is built on it. But do we reckon with it? Does the risen and reigning Christ in fact define our reality? Do we cope with the forces in our lives and in the world around us in the strength of that reality? What would it mean to us if Easter were to capture our minds and hearts as thoroughly as Christmas does?

The Problem

The issue at stake is power, the power that we have, and the power that has us. Compared with our ancestors, we have a lot of power in our human hands. Science and technology have given us comforts, possibilities, and choices beyond the imagination even of aristocrats in previous centuries. Machines are power, and we use them. Money is power, and there is more of it around than ever before. Information is power, and we are flooded with it. Many of us, to be sure, are not content with all of this. Possessions and services that used to be luxuries have become necessities, and we never have quite enough of them. We would like to be both secure and comfortable, and it drives us to search anxiously for ever more money and material goods. We would like just a little more power to control our futures than we have. Through medical science we have made some progress in living longer with less pain, but we would like to conquer both pain and death if we could. Still, never before have so many people (though still a minority of the world's population) had so much power or so many choices in their own hands. We are rulers and dominators, and, on the whole, we act like it.

But power comes at a price. Our lives are reshaped by the requirements of management and control. Machines are not only our servants; they are also our masters. Time moves faster and less of it is our own. Personal community, in family, neighborhood, church, and society, is pressed to the side by the functional demands of a changing work place, and by the drive for a more secure and higher standard of living. Struggle to survive and prosper, using and being driven by the new powers with which we live seems to be our fate. We cannot opt out. Where is God amid all these necessities, hopes, and fears that empower and enslave us in the world we have made?

We also live in a world where impersonal superhuman systems and forces that no one controls drive our history as never before. Armaments — conventional, biochemical, and nuclear — expand despite all treaties. The destruction of our environment proceeds by human enterprise with no regard for the human future. Globalized production, trade, and finance operate by economic laws that can — and often are — used to amass huge profits by those who understand them, with little regard for public welfare. Information technology, spurred by the Internet, blows across all this like a wild wind against which traditional culture can hardly stand, and whose direction no one can direct or predict. The great majority of people around the world who do not have the economic or technological power to participate in these systems are used, destroyed, or simply pushed aside.

All these forces are rooted in human energies and ambitions, but they transcend and dominate human beings. Never in history have we been so completely the creatures of powers in which we participate and from which some of us profit, even while they manipulate and control us.

What does all this have to do with the Christmas, and with Easter? What does it have to do with the power of God? A look again at biblical history might help us here.

The History

The world into which ancient Israel was born knew a great deal about power. Power was the basic reality with which its peoples had to deal. No Platonic vision of justice and the good lifted them to the ideal. No divine-human imperial order placed them in a universal system; indeed, it was in rebellion against the pretensions of such a system in ancient Egypt that Israel was born. Instead, there was a world of competing nations, each with its god and its king, each trying to defend itself against annihilation and to expand its territory and its power. The gods, like the kings, were defined by their power and revered for it. When they failed they could be abandoned for other, more successful deities. Divinity was power, first of all. In the struggle among the gods, that is, among the powers that controlled the world, the question was: Who is almighty?

The answer, in the biblical story, is not some cosmic order that philosophers and priests might seek or some realm beyond being to which the mystic might attain. Nor is it the greatest deity in the sky or the most powerful king on earth. Rather, the Almighty is the One who chose, called, and made a covenant with the people of Israel. *God* did this, not a deity who could be named and whose power could be measured in some imperial, national, or mythical context.

The calling of Moses to lead the Hebrew people out of slavery in Egypt was a dramatic revelation of this God and this relationship. God spoke to Moses out of a burning bush in the desert: "Behold, the cry of the people of Israel has come to me, and I have seen the oppression with which the Egyptians oppress them. Come I will send you to Pharaoh that you may bring forth my people, the sons of Israel, out of Egypt." But Moses demurred. "If I come to the Israelites," he asked, "and say to them, 'The God of your ancestors has sent me to you,' and they ask, 'What is his name?' what shall I say to them?" He expected a name, like Ra or Amon from the Egyptian pantheon, or perhaps Baal from the land of Canaan, a god of proven influence and power. But the reply he received is one of the great revealed mysteries in the Bible, so mysterious that most translations still print it in special type, "I am who I am." It could also be translated, "I will be who I will be" (cf. Exod. 3:7-14).

God did deliver Israel from bondage, through a succession of horrible plagues that finally conquered Pharaoh's resistance. But God was not the servant of Israel's will to power and domination. The covenant God made with the people, the relationship into which God entered with them, was no contractual bargain between a deity and a nation about the use of divine and human power. The claim of this covenant was total; its author was sovereign. Who God is, and who they were, the Hebrew people would come to know as history unfolded — the covenantal history that found its center in Jesus Christ and that will find its consummation in the new heaven and the new earth on the final day.

There is no doubt about the power of God. The Bible is filled with celebrations of it, in the creation of the heavens and the earth, in victory over the wicked and the enemy, in judgment on Israel and the nations. But God's power is not a thing in itself, like the power of electricity or the power of an army. It is not unconditioned formal majesty and omnipotence or naked sovereignty. If it were, the theologian Karl Barth reminds us, God would be a demon and, as such, his own prisoner.[2]

God's power is, by God's own free self-determination, *in* covenant. Who almighty God is; who we are, created, formed, and empowered by God; what the world is, created and determined by God's providential goodness; and what, in God's purpose, is the meaning and direction of all things in history — all this we discover in relationship with God.

2. Barth, *The Humanity of God* (Richmond, Va.: John Knox, 1960), p. 71.

So the very words by which we describe and respond to God change their meaning as the history of this relationship unfolds. God is just. To be just, or "righteous" in traditional language, was, in ancient Hebrew, an expression of power. It meant to be straight, honest, and dependable, and at the same time to fulfill one's nature in action, to be successful, and to prevail. When Pharaoh said to Moses and Aaron after the great plague of hail, "The Lord is righteous and I and my people are wicked" (Exod. 9:27),[3] he was assuming that power and goodness were one and the same. God had the power; therefore God must be in the right.

In a way, Pharaoh was correct. Justice is about power. It is the character of almighty God expressed in covenant with the people. What, then, can we say about it from within that covenant?

I. Justice is defined by the faithfulness and the mercy, the lovingkindness, of God, to whom we owe our existence and our calling.

Justice is rooted not in our human claims on life and on one another but in God's claim on us. In John Calvin's eloquent words:

> We are not our own: let not our reason nor our will, therefore, sway our plans and deeds. We are not our own: let us therefore not set it as our goal to seek what is expedient for us according to the flesh. We are not our own: in so far as we can, let us therefore forget ourselves and all that is ours.
>
> Conversely, we are God's: let us therefore live for him and die for him. We are God's: let his wisdom and will therefore rule all our actions. We are God's: let all the parts of our life accordingly strive toward him as our only lawful goal.[4]

Justice is our guide to what this means in human life. It is not about our desires or interests, nor even in the first place about our

---

3. KJV & RSV translation. The NRSV reads: "The Lord is in the right, and I and my people are in the wrong." The text includes both meanings. To be just *(tsedeq)* or to be wicked *(rasha)* are not only conditions of the soul on the one hand nor good or bad acts on the other. They are ways of understanding and responding to the gift and calling of God.

4. Calvin, *Institutes of the Christian Religion* 3.7.1.

rights, but about the boundless depths and heights of God's concern for us and for all creation.[5] It is the way God's power expresses itself in love. In human terms, it is the way we are called to live for one another and for God. It is not a legal standard, though laws may help define it in particular times and places. It is not the quality of a person, though the practice of faithful obedience may lead one to act justly. It is basically a contribution in a concrete relationship, directed toward affirming other persons as God affirms them, healing relationships that have been broken or damaged.

The biblical David, eventually revered as Israel's greatest king, was not an especially virtuous man. But once, when his enemy Saul was at his mercy, David not only spared Saul but offered him allegiance. Saul, the record says, "lifted up his voice and wept" and said to David, "You are more righteous than I; for you have repaid me good, whereas I have repaid you evil" (1 Sam. 24:16-17). It is the relationship that counts. Justice is the power that builds and heals human community and turns it from self to God.

2. God reaches out for the poor, the weak, and the stranger, to rescue them from oppressors and to bring them into the covenant community.

God's justice is not impartial. It is not the balance of claims in a court of law. It is outrageous partisanship for those in need. The people of Israel had no special virtue when God chose them, brought them out of bondage, and made a covenant with them. They were, in God's words from the book of Deuteronomy, "the fewest of all peoples" (Deut. 7:7). God loved them in their weakness. In the laws that defined that covenant, the poor and the stranger were special objects of concern. The Psalms and the prophetic books in the Old Testament are filled with the cries of the oppressed and the promise of God's redeeming action. "With righteousness he shall judge the poor, and decide with equity for the meek of the earth," promised the prophet Isaiah (11:4), while the psalmist declared:

---

5. Here we are only restating, with relation to the themes of power and justice, what has been more fully set forth in chapter one.

Happy are those whose help is in the God of Jacob,
    whose hope is in the Lord their God,
who made heaven and earth,
    the sea and all that is in them;
who keeps faith forever;
    who executes justice for the oppressed;
    who gives food to the hungry.

The Lord sets the prisoners free;
    the Lord opens the eyes of the blind.
The Lord lifts up those who are bowed down;
    the Lord loves the righteous.
The Lord watches over the strangers;
    he upholds the orphan and the widow,
    but the way of the wicked he brings to ruin. (Psalm 146:5-9)

This is the way of the power of God in human society. It is an open-ended process that aims toward calling, building, and restoring human community in relationship with God.

3. God's justice struggles continually with the injustice of the people of God.

The drama of this struggle fills the whole Old Testament, and the story continues today. Like the people of Israel, we too do not keep the covenant. We shift the focus of our lives from God and God's purposes to our rights, our fears, our desires, and our security. We even use the name and house of God to support our systems and to serve our ends. We do not want the power of a just and merciful God to remold us in its image. We do not trust that power to prevail over the powers of the world, in some of which we have a stake.

But we cannot escape so easily. God's power renews the covenant that we have broken. God judges us for our inhumanity while calling us in forgiveness back into the relationship to which we have been unfaithful. God will give his people "a heart of flesh," so that "they shall be my people, and I will be their God" (Ezek. 11:19-20).

We are not righteous. Our pretensions to be so only magnify our pride and self-conceit, as Jesus made clear more than once in his minis-

85

try (e.g., the story of the Pharisee and the tax collector, Luke 18:9-14), and as we know all too well when we look around us and into our own hearts today.

All this leads to the final break with our self-justification — the death of Christ on the cross. There Christ interceded for us transgressors and bore our sins to their final judgment. There, the powers of this world condemned and executed the power of God.

Let there be no mistake about it: these were not strange alien forces. They are our powers and we belong to them. Jesus had criticized the basic ways of wealth accumulation that we all practice when we can. He had disrupted the moneychangers doing legitimate banking business on which we too depend. He had broken through the taboos that set Samaritans and others outside the national community and thereby threatened some of our communities as well. He had rejected the nationalist hopes of Israel, both religious and revolutionary, and so raised questions about our national identities today. He had poured scorn and anger on the most pious keepers of morality in the culture, which would offend us too, were he to teach in our schools and churches. They were all there in the crowd that howled for his death. With one part of us, we would have been there too. With the other part — our believing, hoping, and now despairing selves — we would have deserted him and fled or, perhaps, with the more honest Peter, wept bitterly. This is how the world is. In our betrayal and our despair, we are part of it.

Then something else happened: something so unexpected, so incredible, so revolutionary, that over two thousand years we have still not probed the depth of its mystery or grasped the fullness of its meaning. The power of God conquered the power of death. The ultimate in human power, execution under the most degrading conditions, could not destroy the sovereign authority of God's justice and love in Jesus. Christ is risen and reigns over all the powers of our unrighteousness. We live now in a new covenant that is a risen form of the old. By grace, by forgiveness, our lives and consciences are really not our own, but Christ's. Our hope is now more than the projection of our longings. It is assurance that we and our world will be transformed by the work of "the Lord, the Spirit" (2 Cor. 3:18). In the words of the apostle Peter, "God has made him both Lord and Messiah, this Jesus whom you crucified" (Acts 2:36).

The Revolution

Today we are living between the times. Christ is risen and reigns. This is the ultimate reality that governs all our understanding, our action, and our hope. The church lives from this reality and proclaims it in word and deed. Yet we live still in a penultimate world looking forward to the coming of Christ. In this world other powers, and other ideas about power, still operate, as they did in the days of the New Testament church.

Some of these powers are the same now as then, though they take different forms. The power of Caesar, of political institutions, laws, and administration, is the most obvious example. Despite the ideas of modern libertarians, we cannot do without governmental power, and despite democracy, it still determines our lives. The power of mammon, of economic activity and the ambiguous motives that drive it, has grown beyond all the proportions of biblical times, but its essence is the same. "Philosophy and empty deceit, . . . according to the elemental spirits of the universe" (Col. 2:8) are still around, though their expressions may today be more ideological and influenced by markets and public opinion research.

Other powers are new, created by the vast scientific expansion of human control over the processes of nature, by new sources of energy, and by the technology of communication. Of them all, however, in the light of the New Testament, certain things may be said.[6]

I. These powers are part of God's creation.

The previous chapter explained in some detail that the powers are created, as the letter to the Colossians in the New Testament puts it, in Christ and for Christ, and they hold together in him (1:16, 17). Knowledge about the powers is not found in some realm outside of God who is revealed to us in the biblical story, who has come on earth in Jesus Christ, and who works among us in the Holy Spirit. The truths that these powers discover, the authority they exercise, and the works they

6. Cf. the further development of this subject in Charles C. West, *Power, Truth and Community in Modern Culture* (Harrisburg, Pa.: Trinity Press International, 1999), ch. 3.

accomplish are not ultimate. In their operations they are not independent enterprises. They are encompassed in God's good providence and in God's mission to fulfill all things in Christ. Their functions in God's purpose are secular, not sacred, in the original and proper meaning of the word "secular." They are concerned with this present age, after the fall and before the final day.[7] They do not reveal God. They are called to serve God by seeking justice, human welfare, and the stewardship of creation amid the relativities of a sinful world, in a way that points toward the coming of Christ.

Government, is not, therefore, evil in and of itself, nor does it exist simply to restrain evil. It is created to be a servant of divine justice, "God's servant for your good" (Rom. 13:4), in its use of law and enforcement in this sinful age before the final day. It may be misused in the service of some other, human lord (the powers of wealth or national pride for example), but this is not its calling.

Similarly, there are no forbidden realms of scientific investigation, as if by probing them we might be threatening God. There is only faithful science that researches the secrets of creation to serve the purposes of God, or unfaithful science that pursues some other objective. There is no realm in which technology may not operate, or where the processes of production, distribution, finance, and exchange may not be developed. There is only responsible technology and just economics that respond to the justice and the covenant love of God, or technology and economics that serve some other purpose.

The Christian church is called, therefore, to affirm these powers in their integrity as God's instruments in this age between Christ's resurrection and his coming in glory. The church does not control them as if it were another human power, but it can by its active witness help them discern and give form to their secular service.

---

7. Cf. "Secularization," in Lossky, Míguez-Bonino, et al., eds., *Dictionary of the Ecumenical Movement* (Grand Rapids: Eerdmans, 1991), pp. 914-18. Here the distinction is made between secularization, the desacralization of this age by the historical work of God, and secularism, a humanist philosophy that rejects God.

2. In this as yet unredeemed world, the powers are not content to serve God.

They seek their own goals; they build their own structures; they establish their own domains. Human ambitions, desires, hopes, and fears are their driving forces, and just because of this they become superhuman systems, demonic spiritual opponents of God that subject human beings to their own domination. This is not a new development. As the account of the tower of Babel in the Bible shows, the urge goes back to the beginning of history: "Come, let us build ourselves a city, and a tower with its top in the heavens, and let us make a name for ourselves; otherwise we shall be scattered abroad upon the face of the whole earth" (Gen. 11:4).

To stand against these powers, both as temptations within and oppressors without, says the apostle Paul, we must put on the whole armor of God: truth, justice, faith, salvation, the sword of the Spirit, and the gospel of peace (Eph. 6:11-17). To serve the mission of God toward the powers, the community of believers is called to resist the powers as they understand and serve themselves, as they make themselves absolute and take the place of God. In one sphere, that of government, Christians have known this since the days of the Roman Caesars. It is just as true in the realm of science as it seeks to control created nature, of technology when it destroys nature or human community, and of an economic system that makes a god of its own profitability.

3. Human beings are caught up in this battle between God and the powers because we are the battleground.

It is our anxiety and fear, our search for pleasure, security, control, and wealth that feeds the rebellion against the covenant. The church knows this most of all, for its members are part of this sinful world. The basic experience of the Christian is to be forgiven, liberated from the sinful self by the sacrifice of Christ, and empowered by the calling and promise of new life in the Spirit who continually transforms us. The community of believers witnesses to this power that judges and changes the world and us. We are stewards of the mysteries of the economy of God in this sinful age as long as it lasts, called to seek the earthly forms of a justice that in ever new ways prepares the way for the coming of Christ.

Put on the whole armor of God, so that you may be able to stand against the wiles of the devil. For our struggle is not against enemies of blood and flesh, but against the rulers, against the authorities, against the cosmic powers of this present darkness, against the spiritual forces of evil in the heavenly places. Therefore take up the whole armor of God, so that you may be able to withstand on that evil day, and having done everything, to stand firm. Stand therefore, and fasten the belt of truth around your waist, and put on the breastplate of righteousness. As shoes for your feet, put on whatever will make you ready to proclaim the gospel of peace. With all of these, take the shield of faith, with which you will be able to quench all the flaming arrows of the evil one. Take the helmet of salvation, and the sword of the Spirit, which is the word of God.

Ephesians 6:11-17

So on the one hand we resist the powers, including those in which we are shareholders, and point toward Christ's victory over them. But in so doing we on the other hand respect the powers in their proper, divinely ordained function. We bear witness to them of the promise that is also theirs, of the plan of God that will finally unite all things in Christ.

The Community

Who then is the church to whom this mission is given? To begin with, let us be clear about a paradox in which we live. On the one hand God defines the church; we do not. The church embraces all those who belong to Christ, everywhere in the world, of whatever communion, even those who, for reasons of doctrine, order, experience, culture, politics, or economic station exclude each other. In the church the whole plurality of the world, with all its conflicts and competitions, is caught up in the household of God whose head is Christ. This household is one community. We must love, listen to, learn from, and be corrected by all of the brothers and sisters in Christ whom God has called to be members of it. Together we confront and bear witness to the global powers that throw us together and at the same time divide us with new systemic structures. The church ecumenical, whenever and however it prays, studies, and acts together, is where this mission happens. We are all part of it.

On the other hand, every congregation in every place, *is* the church of Jesus Christ there. Its mission is to the powers in the particular neighborhood of the world of which it is a part. Local churches should — and often do — penetrate the souls of the neighborhoods, the cities, the businesses, the labor unions, the ethnic groups, and the cultures where they are with the gospel that their living witness brings. Spurred by that same gospel, local congregations often discover a broader community of churches in other neighborhoods, other cultures, with other ways of doctrine and order, and other positions on the economic scale. Here, on the local scene, the same ecumenical encounter takes place as in the world as a whole. The same powers, in another context, are guided toward the purposes of God. The church is one household of God around the world. The church is the body of Christ in every local time and place. Such a church brings the good news to the powers of the world.

The church, therefore, is not a separated community that can pursue its own identity apart from the world's fate. The church is a witness to the world, in the world, of God's coming reign in Christ over the powers of the world. As a believing community it lives in this age, not in some transcendent eternity. As the body of the incarnate, crucified, and risen Christ, it is part of this history where the triune God is at work. There will be no temple in the city of God as the book of Revelation envisions it (21:22) when all is fulfilled. Till then the church is that part of the world that responds in faith, hope, and love to the judgment and promise of God for the world. Its members are engaged in every part of the world's life. We are sent into every sphere of life as the church dispersed, not as individuals. In the family, in the work place, in the community, and in politics we wrestle with the powers to discern, make known, and serve the work of the Spirit and the reign of Christ.

We are, in the words of Paul, stewards of the mysteries of God. We are the shock troops of God's mission.

Finally then, the church is a community that, in its gathered life, brings the world into the presence of God. The church *is* the world, being reconciled to God. In this community, in the power of the Spirit we Christians, worldly sinners that we are, participate in Christ's reconciling reign and learn to be, in the words of the apostle Paul, ambassadors of that reconciliation (2 Cor. 5:20). We hear the judging and saving word of God for the world to which we belong and respond to it. The church is that part of the world which knows and bears witness to the world's creator and redeemer. It is that part of the world which lives in this age with confident hope for what God is already doing and for what God will bring to fulfillment in the age to come. It is that part of the world which takes responsibility for this creation in the light of the new creation that is already here in Christ, "as a plan [Greek: *oikonomia*, or economy] for the fullness of time, to gather up all things in him, things in heaven and things on earth" (Paul to the Ephesians, 1:10).

This witness, this responsibility, is fallible and partial. Church statements on world affairs and the behavior of church members in politics, the marketplace, or even in the family, are not themselves the word or will of God. But they are witnesses amid the powers of this world to the One who is our Lord and theirs. God will both use and correct the church's witness as it is offered in faith, hope, and love.

The Ways of Mission

How, then, in twenty-first-century society, can the church — the whole church, the body of Christ through all its members — practice this responsible witnessing mission? Let us suggest four interacting ways.

1. Analysis

We have, first, a ministry of spiritual analysis. "Beloved, do not believe every spirit," warns the apostle John in his first letter, "but test the spirits to see whether they are from God" (1 John 4:1). It is not easy to probe the subtle complexities of sin in the world. We don't do a very good job of it in our own neighborhoods, in our businesses, or on ourselves. It is much simpler to rail against a demon than to understand him (or her). One need only mention public reaction to the power of drugs or of crime to make the point. It is more comfortable to make friends with a tempter than to see through her (or him). Notice how neatly we rationalize our consumption levels and our standard of living in a world of poverty and need. The devil is enormously clever in misleading us, especially where power is involved. We need, as Paul said, to put on the whole armor of God to resist the devil's wiles. Part of this armor is the sword of the Spirit, which is the word of God (Eph. 6:17), used as an analytical probe.

Our task is to understand the powers of today's world as they really are, not in the oversimplified caricatures that our fears or our desires produce. We need to identify their systemic tendencies, their aims, their driving motivations, and their destructive and constructive effects. We need to perceive how we are involved in their operations. We all need to do this, the church gathered in congregation, synod, or working group, and the church dispersed through all its members where they live and work. Let us look at one massive and obvious example: the powers at work in the globalization of human society.

There was a time, not long ago, when two dominant humanist ideologies competed for the world's allegiance. Both believed that the world was caught up in one revolutionary change. One ideology understood this revolution as boundless expansion of scientific knowledge, technological methods, and industrial production in a competitive free-market world. Individuals would be liberated to pursue their own ends. Wealth would be multiplied, human choices would expand, people of all cultures would be drawn into one society governed by economic exchange. To some degree this did indeed happen. Those of us in the wealthier part of the world, including about 80 percent of Americans, both enjoy the fruits of capitalism and suffer its anxieties every day.

The other ideology saw a growing division of the world into two classes, the capitalist rich, who controlled production and dictated the direction of science and the use of technology, and the increasingly impoverished masses. These poor, the argument went, would progressively lose the last refuges of their humanity, their cultures, and control of the fruits of their labor under capitalist exploitation until, in total revolution, they would replace the power of capital with the power of the people. To some degree this happened as well, producing revolutions that have changed our world.

In time the ideologies modified each other. But on one thing they agreed: the world is one great economic system on which world culture and world society are to be built. Even the Christian church in worldwide mission based itself on this assumption as it tried to challenge both ideological powers with the justice of God, the work of the Spirit, and the reconciling reign of Christ.

Today these ideological visions are gone. Pure communism collapsed in its idealistic illusions about the goodness of people power. Apologies for pure capitalism are still offered, but basically they rationalize the interests of the powers they serve. The reality these visions created, however, is more powerfully at work than ever.

We are caught up in a globalizing process that no vision and no hope encompass. Science and technology are more powerful than ever. To mention only a few examples: agriculture (soil management and genetic alteration), manufacture (automation), pharmaceuticals (miracle drugs), armaments (conventional, nuclear, and biochemical), and communications (Internet and mass media). Research and development in all these fields are driven partly by concern for public good, partly by fear, but mostly by the business enterprises that pay for them and hope to profit from them. So also financial and industrial powers, the transnational corporations and world financial markets, are driven by no coordinated objective except the search for profits, dividends, and capital gains. These institutions in turn are determined by the decisions of millions of investors, including many of us, with the same motives. Finally, political powers, which should be controlling and giving direction to all the others, are themselves embroiled with them, by corruption of their officials, by wealthy special interests that influence elections and legislation, or simply because no national government can by itself restrict or direct international economic and technological power.

The results of this explosion of human power have been transforming and ambivalent. There is far more wealth in the world than ever in history. Millions are living longer, healthier lives and have more freedom of choice than ever before. We can be in instant communication with one another through computers and the media. Awareness of our oneness as a human family is greatly heightened. On the other hand, our industry is slowly destroying the environment in which we live. Chemical pollution is profitable; control of toxic wastes is not. We find it impossible to control the greed for trees, for fish, for fossil fuels and other nonrenewable resources — all of which threatens our ecosystem and upsets our ability to live with the creation God has given us to care for.

Worse, billions of people do not participate in this progress because they live where they do not have access to the systems that drive it or they are unable to pay for its products. The gap between rich and poor is growing wider in the United States and other countries worldwide, while all over the world traditional economies and the cultures based on them are being undermined by the appeal and pressure of new economic powers. Families and villages are breaking up, and people are losing their personal roots as they flock to cities in search of work.

Forces at many levels are at work in this globalizing process. We can recognize some of them in our own lives and communities. The scientist's search for new truth about nature in the laboratory often becomes the desire to control nature, perhaps to cure disease but also to win fame and wealth in doing so. Institutionalized, this becomes the chemical company's financing of research and marketing of a new drug. Where in this picture is God's justice reaching out for the person in need who cannot afford the price?

The shopper's search for well-fitting and inexpensive clothes may drive the clothing firm to improve quality, but at the same time to seek the cheapest labor anywhere in the world to produce the garments. What then turns an Asian sweatshop into a community of God's children?

Banks exist to make profit on interest from their loans. But a family in the community, or a nation in Africa, planning for better times, runs deeply into debt — on a credit card or on an international bank loan. How would the economy of Christ help a debtor with no resources?

In all these cases we cannot too easily label the firm, the manufacturer, or the bank as an evil power. Behind them all are investors, including some of us, who demand that their stock grow and return dividends. Around them are all the forces of competitive enterprise, to which they may succumb. All these powers operate in an economic system that no one finally controls.

These powers involve all of us. None of us who see the news on television or read it in a newspaper can escape them. No member of the church may be indifferent to the witness and the suffering of brothers and sisters in Christ in other parts of the world. Nor may we leave spiritual understanding to experts in finance, technology, and world affairs, Christian or otherwise. We need to understand the powers in all their variety, in their necessities as well as their possibilities, in their systemic requirements and in their effect on real people, if we, who are all together and each personally, the church, are to minister to them in Christ's name.

Together we are all theological analysts in the body of Christ, trying to understand the society around us in the light of God's judgment and redemption. So we respond in common study of the word of God and of the society around us, to discover together what God is doing in this world and what the form of our discipleship should be. We are the world listening and responding to God.

We do this at all levels of the church. The Roman Catholic Church is guided by papal encyclicals on social questions, and by a Pontifical Commission on Justice and Peace. Protestant and Orthodox Christians struggle together in the World Council of Churches for a common understanding of Christian social witness. On a national level the same common search goes on both among and within denominations, as well as among groups that represent various causes and communities in the church and world. Nor are local congregations and communities outside this ministry. The powers affect our lives wherever we live: in the businesses where we work and with which we deal, in the schools our children attend, in the way our neighborhoods are structured and changed, and in the local governments that make and enforce our laws.

In dealing with them all, neither Christians nor their churches are infallible. We are faithful theological analysts, that is all. This is our "spiritual worship" (Rom. 12:1). We proclaim the word of God that judges and changes us all. But in this ministry the powers of this age are all, on every level, our responsibility. They are the field of our mission.

2. Intercession

But we are not only analysts. Our question concerns faithful living and faithful witness.

To this belongs, secondly, a ministry of intercession. Karl Barth calls intercession, with relation to the power of government, a priestly ministry that all Christian citizens in a democratic society are called to perform.[8] How are the powers of this world called to serve the purposes of God? This is not a question to be answered with some ideal picture, painted in a church meeting room. We can only find an answer when the church community accompanies its members into the realms in which these powers operate, with counseling and with prayer.

Church members need help and support from each other in discerning how, in all the places where we separately live and work among the powers of the world, we should understand and serve the Christ whose reign is present and coming. We may need help in understanding the power systems in which we are caught, in order better to deal with them. We may need support in sustaining the service to which we are called, when financial insecurity or sacrifice threatens. We may need the backing of the community in resisting a power, at risk of losing a job or worse. We may need the guidance and correction of the community when our own fears or ambitions pull us into serving those powers instead of the justice of God. In all of this, the church gathers us all into a community that is not of the world, but for the world in Christ. For example:

A. *The banking system is essential to us all.* The services it performs, in offering credit and handling exchanges of money, are clear. But a bank, to perform these services, must take risks with loans and build its reserves to cover those risks. To serve this end, in our economy, small banks with less margin are being bought out by larger ones. Loan policies are becoming less accommodating to the debtor in time of need, and more impersonally efficient in determining credit rating. Those who suffer are the small depositors with lower income, and often certain minorities as a group. How big should a bank be and how does its size affect its loan policies and choice of customers? What is a proper balance between the search for profit and stability on the one side and service to all in need on the other? Already on the international scene the World Bank is facing this problem with its loans to poorer nations. In an echo of the biblical year of jubilee, some debts have been forgiven, and stringent requirements for the reform of national economies have been relaxed. Can this be good banking practice and a witness to the coming of God's economy as well?

---

8. *Church and State* (London: Student Christian Movement Press, 1939), p. 66.

B. *Technological developments in production, transportation, communication, and every area of the common life have changed our civilization.* They have arisen to meet needs in the countries with most advanced development. They serve us all, but especially those who can pay for their advantages. Private cars have developed further than public transportation. Luxury homes are more easily built than low-cost housing. Suburbs flourish and cities decay, or are "gentrified," driving out the poor. One could multiply the examples. Sharpest, however, is the difference between countries that have and those that have not "developed." Yet these poorer countries could profit as much from technology as developed ones, if that technology were applied to their needs. What is appropriate technology for the common good and the benefit of the poor? How might it be directed and financed?

C. *Much has been made of the benefits of free world trade in expanding markets and raising standards of living.* It is an overwhelming power in the world today and it has indeed done much good. We cannot, if we would, return to closed national economies. But once again economic enterprises seeking profits look for the lowest production costs and the highest prices, regardless of human consequences or the fate of the natural environment. Manufacturers have moved their operations from Europe and the United States to low-wage countries where working conditions are poor, labor cannot bargain collectively, and pollution laws, if they exist, are not enforced. Furthermore, international producers squeeze out local businesses in poorer countries by flooding the market with standardized, sometimes lower-cost, products. What might a manufacturing and trading policy look like that would be economically viable, yet responsible and humane?

To all of this we respond with a ministry of corporate intercession, informed by the corporate analysis of the church, that guides our understanding of how the Spirit may be at work among all these powers and how we as members of the church are called to be priests to our neighbors there. We examine our subservience to the powers of the world, our failures in discipleship and witness, and we confess our sins. We bring the dilemmas of our involvement with those powers — in our communities, in the education of our children, in our choices as consumers, in our professions and daily work, in our investments if we have any, and at times in our politics — to God in prayer for guidance. We intercede for the world — for the victims of the power of others, for those in responsible positions as stewards of human power — and for justice, peace, and the common good. We give praise and thanks for the work of the Spirit in the midst of daily events, for the serving witness of the faithful (whether they are Christian or not), and for signs of the coming victory of Christ that will bring all the powers of the world under his reign in God's economy. We do this among ourselves, in the community of the church. We do it in the world where we live and work, by the way we participate with all our neighbors in guiding the powers toward building a just and human society.

3. Prophecy

Third, we are not only priests and intercessors. We also have a prophetic ministry of witness and influence. We must be careful with this responsibility. We are not managers of the global economy, as if from some Christian office we could send out directives to those in the field. This has been the problem with too many church statements on social issues. The church has no political power, and no influence other than that which Christ himself can exercise. We are sinful participants in the world of earthly powers. As such we can only witness to the judgment of God on the injustices from which we also profit and to the promise of God for those who renounce unjust power and seek new and more just relations with their neighbors.

We speak first to ourselves and therefore to the world. We are the ones first called to repentance and therefore to a strategy of action. Church people's participation in the southern freedom marches a generation ago was probably a more effective witness to Christ's reign than all church preaching to the world on the subject of race. When we can go to a secular group working for human justice or environmental responsibility and say: "My church believes this, and therefore I am here," we are more credible witnesses than any document.

We are not managers. But as prophets we are in the business of both protest and influence. We may have to be protesters in the name of Christ, even at the risk of being one-sided. The recent and ongoing campaign of the churches for international debt relief is a good example. One could argue the merits of such relief and the conditions that should attend it. But in this case the financial power of the world faces peoples so poor they cannot sustain their economies, to say nothing of paying their debts. This is a time to confront the powers on behalf of the poor, not mediate between them. There can be other such times. The civil rights struggle of the 1960s was one of them.

But protest is a tactic, not an end in itself. It leads to interaction, to influence the powers toward justice and responsibility for the common good. On a national level the Interfaith Center for Corporate Responsibility is a good example. It monitors the behavior of large corporations, for example in environmental policy, labor relations, treatment of minorities, conditions in the workplace, and influence on public welfare. Sometimes it brings shareholder resolutions on behalf of the churches. They are a minor gesture. If they get 3 percent of the vote, they are enormously successful. But this is enough to bring a corporation into a conversation that can lead to changes in its way of doing business. Influence is also witness. It can happen in other places as well.

We bear our witness as a community that is both prophetic and pastoral. In our day prophecy can take many forms. In councils local, national, or world, we may formulate and proclaim a word of the church to the powers — a call to repentance, to justice, or to the meeting of human need — recognizing that it is a word to ourselves as well. We can and should do the same as congregations in our local communities where the powers of special interest threaten our schools, our peace, or the poor who live among us. In analysis and advocacy we can and must confront the powers of the world, their motives, their ideologies, and their actions, with the word of God. As stewards of the gifts of God and witnesses to the reign of Christ, we participate in the search for just social policy and the common good with, and if need be against, the interests of the powerful.

Prophetic ministry of this kind is not always successful ministry. It is the crucified Christ who reigns. The powers often prevail in this as yet unredeemed world. Martin Luther King Jr. was assassinated in a struggle against the racism that still pervades our culture. The church in other parts of the world, confronted with political, economic, or religious oppression — in Egypt, in Sudan, in parts of China, India, Indonesia, and Latin America for example — know the strength of these powers better than do most Americans. The test of true prophecy, of true witness to the reign of Christ, is not its success but its faithfulness in confronting the powers. Many unsung believers, in lives of suffering and sacrifice, have borne and still bear this witness against, and for the sake of, their persecutors.

But this prophecy grows out of, and is nourished by, the life of the community itself in Christ. God has called the church to be a prophetic *community*. The love which binds members of a congregation to one another in all their faults, virtues, strengths, and weaknesses, is, like Christ himself, transforming and inclusive. It has been a mark of vital Christian community since the earliest days of the church. It is also a love that reaches beyond the local group. It crosses boundaries of class and culture to other societies and to the other side of the street, concerning itself with people on the margin everywhere, working to bring them justice and sharing with them the saving grace of life in Christ. When our vision thus extends this transforming love to more of the human family than those present in our own congregations, it leads to prophecy.

The church's prophetic witness against social evil, its stance of resistance and stewardship toward worldly powers, does not arise, then, out of abstract concern for a just order. It is part of our pastoral concern as Christians for all the people for whom Christ died. It is a sign of the coming reign of God. It expresses the hope we are given, in the "economy of the mystery hidden for ages in God who created all things" and which will be realized in Christ (Eph. 3:9).

4. Imagination

Finally, the church owes the powers of the world a ministry of social imagination. Now more than ever the world needs a vision of realizable justice, expressed in the church. Elements of it might be:

A. *A world community of responsible relationships that transcends nations and cultures and gives them a creative place in the economy of God.* Today the global powers are playing havoc with traditional communities. Village cultures around the world are being impoverished. Millions of people are flocking to large cities in search of work, forced into patterns of life that traditional family and community customs and morals do not control. Meanwhile, a new culture, dictated by the requirements of technology and financial enterprise, standardized by mass media, permeates most of the countries of the world. Some are caught up in it and profit from its affluence. Others are pushed by it into more intense poverty and insecurity.

The church of Jesus Christ was global long before the powers of finance and business were, and everywhere throughout history it has affirmed and cultivated the cultures into which it has come. To be sure, it has at times become the vehicle of one culture over against another. One need only mention Polish Catholics vs. Russian Orthodox in the Middle Ages or Protestant vs. Catholic in Northern Ireland today. But this was not, and is not, the church's gospel, as world mission in modern times and the ecumenical movement in the past century have powerfully demonstrated. We are Christians of many cultures. We confess the faith in many ways, practice many varieties of liturgy, and order our churches differently. This variety expresses the fullness of the Spirit through which we learn from one another to grow in grace. But we all know, with Paul the Apostle, that "there is one body and one Spirit, just as you were called to the one hope of your calling, one Lord, one faith, one baptism, one God and Father of us all" (Eph. 4:4-6). Therefore we cannot break community with one another, however deep our differences are. Unity in Christ is given us and through us to the world, as the basis of our lives together and as a promise for all our nations and our cultures. The vision of the ecumenical movement, inadequately but really expressed in the World Council of Churches and countless other communities of prayer, study, and witness across confessional lines, was never so needed as now, as a call to the churches and a model for the world.

B. *A local community that cultivates human freedom for all in the context of mutual responsibility, including the disabled and the poor.* One of the casualties both of humanist ideology and of globalizing powers has been the growth of individualism at the cost of mutuality. But in Christ we are bound to one another in the liberating bond of love that reaches out to all our neighbors. To live this, sometimes in defiance of the pressures of competition and the need for security, would re-create in this world a reality that would have its own, quite worldly, power.

C. *The cultivation of life goals in terms of quality of relationships, not quantities of power or possession.* We have become obsessed with quantity in today's world. Scientific truths are expressed in quantitative terms. We have so much more power and so many more possessions than our ancestors did that power and possessions have become a way of life. We can only understand the economy in terms of its expansion and progress in terms of a higher standard of living. The qualities of human life — the infinite varieties of human interaction, with nature and with each other — have been submerged in our striving. But the reign of Christ is about relationships. It matures by sanctification, not by accomplishment. It leads us into a community where each is indeed a limit to the other, but a limit that affirms and gives life to the other in love, the expansion of whose possibilities are unbounded. This is the reality we are given, which we do not need to achieve, but which we are invited to explore with all the fullness of our being. This vision, should we practice it, could be a liberation for the world around us.

D. *The embodiment of a community in which justice is leavened with forgiveness and love.* This should, of course, be the standard for all society. Justice that tries to stand by itself degrades into injustice. It becomes the instrument of one power against another, or at best the compromise of their interests. The justice of God, as we have seen, is not that. It is the form of the unbounded loving-kindness of God in covenant with the people. It reaches out to rescue, to uphold and establish the poor, the disabled, and the sinner. Ultimately it justifies us by forgiving grace in Christ and brings us as new creations into community with him. This is the message of the power of God that the powers of the world are waiting for. To practice this justice in the Christian community is our most powerful witness of all.

5

PRACTICES

Reoriented in the Way of Christ

> *Come to me, all you that are weary and are carrying heavy burdens, and I will give you rest. Take my yoke upon you, and learn from me; for I am gentle and humble in heart, and you will find rest for your souls. For my yoke is easy, and my burden is light.*
> MATTHEW 11:28-30

M uch time, energy, and money is being expended today to help the church become more relevant and accessible, to make its message and services attractive, understandable, and inviting. Shaped by the images and expectations of contemporary culture, the church has become a vendor of religious goods and services. Seeking to be sensitive to the hurts and hopes of "secular" or "non-churched" people, and/or to be responsive to the needs and desires of the "person in the pew," the church all too often uncritically accommodates itself to current cultural trends. As illustrated in earlier chapters, the understanding of the gospel itself then takes on a consumer-oriented marketing slant: promoting the benefits to be received, furnishing answers to pressing questions, providing remedies to various ills, offering a new life to be enjoyed, or promising a future state to be secured.

In contrast, the gospel Jesus proclaims contains not only a promise but also a summons. It is both gift and challenge. The gift is nothing less than new life. The challenge is that that new life is offered within the context of a relationship of radical trust in God and radical obedience to the way of Christ. The summons to take up this relationship, this challenge, is perhaps most clearly heard in the verses in Matthew 5 known as the Beatitudes.

These often-studied verses form the powerful introduction to Jesus' "Sermon on the Mount" within the Gospel of Matthew, and they stand in mystifying contrast to our habits of mind. Far from attempting to discern and meet the self-defined needs of the people who came to hear him, as might happen in a consumer culture, Jesus here confronts and reframes human concerns and expectations. The issue becomes not benefits to be received, but conversion: a change of mind, a change of actions and relationships, a total reorientation of life. God does indeed bless human life, but the blessings of the reign of God flow out of a new relationship with God that is expressed in radical discipleship. The call is to hear the teachings of Jesus — to learn from him — and, forsaking all other obligations and loyalties, to trust and follow only him.

That is why being the church — a disciple community — is not about personal fulfillment and self-interest, the meeting of individual needs, or the pursuit of happiness, success, and moral justification. Taking on the yoke of Jesus Christ entails nothing less than a new way of living in the world. But read the verses that open this chapter once again. Jesus does not offer a yoke heavy with impossible expectations. Instead, he offers himself as rest; his yoke as the way of ease. The burden we place on ourselves — the misguided weight of all that we think we want and need — that burden is heavy indeed. By contrast, Jesus, the compassionate teacher, offers another way: a life of gratitude and obedience, of service and sacrifice, of celebration and commitment, of freedom and responsibility. In its wholeness, it provides rest for those who participate in that way of life. In the Beatitudes we can trace the shape of such an unencumbered community. It is to them that we now turn our attention as we seek a new vision of what the church is and can yet become.

Communal Guidance

When Jesus saw the crowds, he went up to the mountain; and after he sat down, his disciples came to him. Then he began to speak, and taught them, saying . . .

MATT. 5:1-2

Throughout the history of the Christian tradition, the Gospel of Matthew has been considered the "Book of the Church." A study of the overall perspective and themes reveals an overriding concern for the life and practice of the community of faith. Not only is this the only gospel to use the term "church" *(ekklesia)*, but both its content and structure reveal a strong interest in providing clear and coherent guidance for the identity and integrity of the new communities formed around Jesus Christ. Within Matthew's framework, the Beatitudes are not sayings about private individual moral character. Instead, they describe the quality of life and witness of communities whose members have heard the Good News — the proclamation of the new life to be found in relationship with Jesus Christ — and are living in the new reality this gospel brings forth. Rather than general rules for living, the Beatitudes offer instruction, wisdom, and guidance specifically for the disciple community, for those participating in the liberating reign of God. Indeed, embodying or performing the way of life expressed by the Beatitudes requires a communal life of mutual support and encouragement: "Whether or not the new ethic can be fulfilled is something that can only be determined by groups of people who consciously place themselves under the gospel of the reign of God and wish to be real communities of brothers and sisters — communities which form a living arena of faith and journey together as the people of God."[1]

Blessed Are Those Who . . .

Too often the Beatitudes have led a disembodied life unconnected to their context. Lifted from the fuller setting of Matthew's gospel, they

---

1. Gerhard Lohfink, *Jesus and Community: The Social Dimension of Christian Faith* (Minneapolis: Fortress Press, 1984), p. 62.

become pithy sayings, almost slogans, that remind Christians what they *ought* to be about. Rather than describing new life within the reign of God, "[t]hey become new rules and as rules they eventually produce the predictable forms of ethical activism, anguish, or security — depending upon the species of self-deception at work in the hearer."[2] Focusing upon the individual and his or her well-being, the Beatitudes are interpreted either (1) as personal comfort, indicating that if you are poor or persecuted or hungry, God will provide for you; or (2) as moral commands to show mercy, be peacemakers, and seek righteousness in order to find favor in the sight of God.

When in the Beatitudes Matthew records Jesus' use of the language pattern, "Blessed are those who . . . ," he was using a formula that would have had a recognizable ring in the ears of those familiar with the Old Testament scriptures. But Jesus placed the words within a new framework. When Jesus said, "Blessed are those . . . ," he was announcing the sovereign reign of God. In the context of Jesus' healing, teaching, and preaching ministry, the relationship with God and the understanding of God's blessings upon his people receive an interpretation that goes beyond traditional expectations:

> To his Palestinian peers, Jesus must have sounded as if he were saying, in effect: "Happy the poor, the hungry, the mourning; the more you know your need for God, the more you shall be open to God's end-time Reign, which is beginning to happen already — in my healing, my teaching, and in my gathering of the outcast in table fellowship."[3]

The Beatitudes turn a spotlight on those who are the special objects of God's determined action, those who will participate in the wholeness and goodness of life within the reign of God.

The Beatitudes paint a portrait of a disciple community living within — performing — the gospel, a community committed to basing its life on the promise of God's kingdom. "This is what the life of those who stand in the salvation time of God is like, of those who are freed

---

2. Richard Lischer, "The Sermon on the Mount as Radical Pastoral Care," *Interpretation* 41 (1987): 161.

3. Dennis Hamm, *The Beatitudes in Context: What Luke and Matthew Meant* (Wilmington, Del.: Michael Glazier, 1990), p. 25.

When Jesus saw the crowds, he went up the mountain; and after he sat down, his disciples came to him. Then he began to speak, and taught them, saying:

"Blessed are the poor in spirit, for theirs is the kingdom of heaven.

"Blessed are those who mourn, for they will be comforted.

"Blessed are the meek, for they will inherit the earth.

"Blessed are those who hunger and thirst for righteousness, for they will be filled.

"Blessed are the merciful, for they will receive mercy.

"Blessed are the pure in heart, for they will see God.

"Blessed are the peacemakers, for they will be called children of God.

"Blessed are those who are persecuted for righteousness' sake, for theirs is the kingdom of heaven.

"Blessed are you when people revile you and persecute you and utter all kinds of evil against you falsely on my account. Rejoice and be glad, for your reward is great in heaven, for in the same way they persecuted the prophets who were before you."

Matthew 5:1-12

from the power of Satan, and in whom the wonder of discipleship is consummated."[4] Thus Jesus' instructions concerning the manner of life of his disciples have the character of pastoral care (support and guidance based upon God's redemptive reality), rather than rules (imposed mandates and regulations dependent upon human achievement).

---

4. Joachim Jeremias, *The Sermon on the Mount* (London: Athlone Press, 1961), p. 29.

The Life and Witness of the Church

Like the gospel itself, the quality of communal life and practice described by the Beatitudes is both gift and promise. On the one hand, through the ministry, death, and resurrection of Jesus Christ, the new way of life within God's reign already exists — it is an experienced reality. On the other hand, until the fullness of God's kingdom of peace, love, and justice is consummated, the transformed way of life indicated by the Beatitudes is a future reality hoped and prayed for — an expectation to be realized.

> The Beatitudes characterize those who have been called by God. They are less a roll call of kingdom-virtues than an affirmation of the eschatological blessedness which is already enjoyed by those who are followers of Jesus Christ. The Beatitudes are not a strategy or exhortation but an indicative with the force of a promise. So sure is the reality of the kingdom which has been inaugurated by Jesus that his followers already have what the kingdom promises.[5]

This eschatological dimension — that God's reign is "already" and at the same time "not yet" — signifies the importance of the church. The community of God's people proclaims and embodies an alternative identity and vision.

> The church is "first fruits": i.e., it is to be in itself the beginning of what is to come. This means both that the church's presence constitutes a part of the promise that more is to come (what is meant by the biblical word "earnest"); but also that its quality and direction have begun to be manifest. The church does communicate to the world what God plans to do, because it shows that God is beginning to do it.[6]

The astonishing claims made about the church in the Gospel of Matthew: "You are the salt of the earth. . . . You are the light of the world" (5:13-14) are not due to the church's wisdom, piety, or goodness

---

5. Lischer, "The Sermon on the Mount as Radical Pastoral Care," p. 160.

6. John Howard Yoder, "Why Ecclesiology Is Social Ethics," in *The Royal Priesthood: Essays Ecclesiological and Ecumenical* (Grand Rapids: Eerdmans, 1994), p. 126.

but to its redemptive relationship with Jesus Christ. A community that has died and risen with Christ is freed from the desire to secure and protect its own life and well-being. The confidence to challenge the established way of the world is due to the belief that Jesus has made a difference: in him God's saving future has invaded the present. Through his words and actions, the promised kingdom has been inaugurated. God's liberating and invigorating new social order has begun. The calling of the church is to be a real, visible, tangible, capable of being experienced — though not yet perfected — actualization of the reign of God in the world.

> As a body of disciples and beginners, taken on by grace and forgiveness, the church touches and experiences the beginnings of the "new thing" which God is doing — and does so because, in Christ, this "new thing" is already accomplished. . . . Not only by proclamation but also by deed, the church is called to let God's Kingdom show in the world and for the world — to give the world a taste, an inkling, of "the glory which shall be revealed."[7]

Followers of Christ do not interpret their covenantal relationship with God through external statutes and ordinances but through the person of Jesus Christ. Their obedience to God is not accomplished through dutiful human achievement, but it is offered in faithful relationship with Jesus Christ. This relationship is made visible to the world as Christ's disciples participate in the community of those who would follow Jesus. The new creation, the new way of life in God's kingdom, is already a reality within the life of the community of Jesus' disciples. And as this community assumes the yoke of Jesus — the promise and the summons of his way of life — it participates in the blessedness of a covenant relationship with God. Living within this relationship, watching for and welcoming the signs of God's reign that it sees in its own life, the community discovers its true purpose: to participate in God's redemptive mission in the world.

The Evangelist Matthew interpreted and proclaimed the gospel of Jesus Christ to a church seeking to discover its identity and calling in changing circumstances. He attempted to illuminate the distinctive life

---

7. *For the Sake of the Kingdom: God's Church and the New Creation* (London: Inter-Anglican Theological and Doctrinal Commission, 1986), p. 23.

and witness of the disciple community. This is the significance and the intent of the Sermon on the Mount. In order to hear the familiar words of the Beatitudes in some new ways, the following discussion will group the eight Beatitudes into four pairs and relate them to the central themes of Matthew's Gospel. These themes give both content and shape to the church's performance of the good news of Jesus Christ.

A People Trusting in God: The Poor and the Meek

The authentic life and witness of the disciple community is not found in obedience to abstract principles, laws, or rules, but in faithfully following the path set by a particular individual — Jesus of Nazareth. In the life and ministry of Jesus the Messiah, Israel's hopes for restoration and salvation have been fulfilled. In him the sovereign God has drawn near to dwell with God's people, and life as God intends it to be has begun. At the very beginning of his Gospel, Matthew establishes Jesus as the one whose very name means that he "will save his people from their sins" (Matt. 1:21) and as "Emanuel," which means "God with us" (1:23).

Matthew's proclamation of Jesus as Messiah takes its theme from the prophecy of Isaiah 40-55, in which Isaiah calls the expected Messiah the Suffering Servant of the Lord. Isaiah 42:1-4, while found explicitly but once in Matthew (Matt. 12:18-21), "is tantamount to a summary of the ministry of Jesus Messiah, here called 'Servant.'"[8] God does not establish justice and salvation in the accepted and expected manner of the world — violence, control, and domination — but through humble, quiet, and suffering service. Yet, because Jesus fulfills the prophecy of Isaiah 42, his life and death, precisely in their "lowliness," do not show passive acceptance, but rather dynamic obedience. Rather than relying upon his own wisdom and strength, Jesus emptied himself and entrusted his life and destiny to the God of Israel.

Jesus' exchange with Peter in Matthew 16 illustrates this turnaround in messianic expectations. In response to the question, "Who do you say that I am?" Peter gives the right answer, "You are the Messiah, the Son of the living God" (Matt. 16:16). Yet when Jesus goes on to

8. Jack Kingsbury, *Matthew: Structure, Christology, Kingdom* (Minneapolis: Fortress Press, 1975), p. 103.

describe the path he must follow, Peter responds, "God forbid it, Lord!" (Matt. 16:22). Then, as now, human dreams of success and fulfillment are a hindrance to Jesus' mission. His messianic realization through an obedient trust in God's will, even as it led to death, remains a corrective to all popular expectations. Jesus, the Messiah, "[brought] forth justice to the nations" (Isa. 42:1), not through force but as a faithful servant, the trusting one to whom God's Spirit is given, even in suffering. The community that follows this Messiah is called to the same trust.

Blessed Are the Poor in Spirit

"Jesus announces his eschatological blessings to those who stand before God empty-handed and destitute, who seek from him a new relationship with God as well as with others, who come open to God's mercy and forgiveness with integrity, and who desire to experience and establish *shalom*."[9]

The world calls human beings to place their trust in many things: their intellect, their material wealth, or their physical prowess. The multitude of self-help programs lead to the expectation that people can make their own way and be successful if they just try hard enough. And self-help programs don't only shape the lives of individuals. There are many such programs for churches as well — how to attract more members, more volunteers, more money, more influence. The same attitude that shapes our lives as individuals also shapes the ministries of churches. Rather than standing empty before God, seeking God's mercy and forgiveness, members of the faith community attempt to own and direct their own lives, to determine their own destinies.

Matthew presents a very different picture. The only way to find life as God intends it (whether personally or as a community) is to lose our lives, to give up everything that blocks total dependence upon God. The pride of self-reliance, self-sufficiency, and self-control is a barrier to participation in the goodness and wholeness of life inaugurated by the humble obedience of Jesus the Messiah. The kingdom of heaven is not given to the proud in spirit but to the poor in spirit.

9. Robert Guelich, *The Sermon on the Mount: A Foundation for Understanding* (Dallas: Word, 1982), pp. 29-30.

In keeping with his depiction of Jesus as the fulfillment of Israel's messianic expectations, Matthew aligns the Beatitudes with the prophecy of Isaiah 61. Thus "the poor in spirit" whom God blesses are those whose hope is flagging — "the brokenhearted" (Isa. 61:1). While these persons may be poor in material ways, it includes those who are impoverished in a subtler yet still significant manner, for example, those who are poverty-stricken in the very energy of life — having a weary or "faint" spirit (Isa. 61:3). Matthew stresses the relationship of those who are "poor" with God, rather than those who are economically deprived. The poor are those who can no longer rely upon their own resources, who come empty-handed, who know their need for God. They can no longer trust in their own resources, but only in God. "The 'poor in spirit' are those who stand without pretense before God, stripped of all self-sufficiency, self-security, and self-righteousness."[10]

It was not the strong and proud of Jewish society but the social and religious outcasts — the sick, the sinners, the dispossessed — who were drawn to Jesus, who recognized that God was at work in him. No longer basing their lives in what they owned or controlled, they turned to God and sought to live out of God's "wealth of spirit." The Suffering Servant bore the burdens of the poor in spirit and through his healing and teaching called them into a new relationship of blessing with God here and now: "for theirs is the kingdom of heaven" (Matt. 5:3).

Blessed Are the Meek

The meek are among the poor in spirit. They are those who in their distress can expect nothing from the world; therefore, they look toward and cast themselves upon God. "The meek are those afflicted, who, in their affliction, do not take it upon themselves to seek redress or to overthrow the oppressor, but wait upon God's deliverance."[11] For Matthew, Jesus models the way of the meek in his acceptance of his lowliness: "Behold, your king is coming to you, humble, and mounted on a donkey" (Matt. 21:5). He also calls his disciples to share his affliction

---

10. Guelich, *The Sermon on the Mount,* p. 98.

11. Gene L. Davenport, *Into the Darkness: Discipleship in the Sermon on the Mount* (Nashville: Abingdon, 1988), p. 63.

and his meekness, "Take my yoke upon you . . . for I am gentle and humble in heart" (Matt. 11:29). As Jesus is not self-willed, but trusts in God's will, so can those who are afflicted — if they come and follow him — learn to rely upon God for their eventual deliverance. And just as Jesus' humbleness does not arise out of passivity but active obedience, the way of the meek is not to be equated with quietism (although that may sometimes be an appropriate expression); it is simply the determination to be about the life of discipleship trusting in and waiting upon God.

Matthew's blessing of the meek, "for they will inherit the earth," is nearly a verbatim quotation from Psalm 37. Focusing on the religious problem of social injustice, the psalmist calls for the righteous, those oppressed by the wicked, to "trust in the Lord," "take delight in the Lord," "commit your way to the Lord," "be still before the Lord," and to "refrain from anger, and forsake wrath!" But they are not called simply to accept their fate and put up with intolerable conditions, for the psalmist goes on to declare that God will vindicate the faithful: "the meek shall inherit the land, and delight themselves in abundant prosperity" (Ps. 37:11). Not a glossing over of suffering and oppression, an approval of the status quo, or a law against change, Matthew's beatitude, as the psalm, is a pledge, a trust in and assurance of God's faithfulness. The Promised Land — participation in God's transformation of all earthly life — will be given to the waiting, the lacking, the lowly, the empty before God. Thus Matthew's constant exhortation to the doing of God's will and the threat of judgment upon the disobedient lead not to reliance upon human actions, but to trust in the inbreaking redemptive reign of God manifested and rendered accessible to "the poor in spirit" and "the meek" in the way of Jesus the Messiah.

As the disciple community learns this trust, it will refuse to carry out in its life the oppression of the society of which it is part. It will honor those gifted with spiritual, not material, wealth. It will welcome people of all sizes, colors, and classes. As the community deepens in trust and in the freedom of this new way of life, it will become a place remarkably different from other social organizations. It will also become a seedbed of justice, whose sprouts will pop up in the workplaces and neighborhoods surrounding it, as well as in places far removed from its sanctuary.

Becoming a people of trust, a people poor in spirit and meek, will not come naturally. The practice of prayer is at the heart of forming

Do not fret because of the wicked;
    do not be envious of wrongdoers,
for they will soon fade like the grass,
    and wither like the green herb.
Trust in the LORD, and do good;
    so you will live in the land, and enjoy security.
Take delight in the LORD,
    and he will give you the desires of your heart.

Commit your way to the LORD;
    trust in him, and he will act.
He will make your vindication shine like the light,
    and the justice of your cause like the noonday.

Be still before the LORD, and wait patiently for him;
    do not fret over those who prosper in their way,
    over those who carry out evil devices.

Refrain from anger, and forsake wrath.
    Do not fret — it leads only to evil.
For the wicked shall be cut off,
    but those who wait for the LORD shall inherit the land.

Yet a little while, and the wicked will be no more;
    though you look diligently for their place,
        they will not be there.
But the meek shall inherit the land,
    and delight themselves in abundant prosperity.

Psalm 37:1-11

communities who are able to trust in and be assured of God's faithfulness. As disciples of Jesus the Messiah, Christians pray "in Jesus' name," for it is only through faith in him that we can know and be in relationship with God. Christian prayer is shaped by the prayer Jesus taught the disciples, the Lord's Prayer (Matt. 6:9-13). To pray the Lord's Prayer is a dangerous activity. True prayer is life-creating and life-changing. As a community prays, "Thy will be done," it opens itself to God's testing and to God's purposes.

As a celebration of the gift and call of the new life of trust, a community could not do better than to pray the Lord's Prayer continually, thoughtfully, and with hearts willing to follow its lead. This prayer refocuses our attention from all efforts to secure our lives and well-being to the central issues of God's kingdom. Rather than wealth and accomplishment, the Lord's Prayer lifts up the basics of human life: daily bread, forgiveness, and deliverance from temptation. Prayer shapes a people humble in their habits, steadfast in their faith, modest in their words, just in their actions, merciful in their dealings, and disciplined in their conduct.[12] Such a people trust only in the God made present in the life and death of Jesus, "for theirs is the kingdom of heaven."

A People Hoping in God's Kingdom:
The Mourners and the Merciful

The core of Jesus' gospel is the declaration that "the kingdom of Heaven has come near" (Matt. 4:17). The promise and the hope of the kingdom, of God's rule or reign, shapes the whole of the Gospel of Matthew. The beginning of Jesus' activity in Galilee (Matt. 4:12-25) sets the tone for his ministry. Announcing that the kingdom is at hand, God's rule becomes a living reality in and through his preaching, teaching, and healing. In Jesus the Messiah, God draws near to be with God's people. Into the stormy darkness of the old age of sin, death, and the law, the light of God's new age of forgiveness, life, and the gospel is now shining. While waiting for the final consummation of God's reign,

---

12. Cyprian of Carthage, "On the Lord's Prayer," *The Ante-Nicene Fathers,* vol. 5, p. 451.

those who follow Jesus Christ can live in hope, for the kingdom has come into their midst: "the people who sat in darkness have seen a great light" (Matt. 4:16). Those who "strive first for the kingdom of God and his righteousness" (Matt. 6:33) and pray for God's will to be done "on earth as it is in heaven" (Matt. 6:10) enjoy even now the blessings of God's gracious rule.

Blessed Are Those Who Mourn

The imagery of the new age in the midst of the old age, or of the light illuminating the darkness, illustrates the paradox or tension of Christian life. While the struggle and pain of earthly reality have not passed away, their power to determine the meaning and purpose of human life has been overcome in the cross and resurrection of Jesus Christ. Those who "mourn" recognize both the joy of the new age and the tragedy of the old. They express the bereavement that is part and parcel of this time "in between." "The proclamation of blessedness to those who mourn heralds the turning point in God's relation to the creation. To *all* who agonize over the crippling, destroying impact of the Old Age, to *all* who mourn over the rampancy of the Power of Death in the creation, Jesus proclaims God's dependability, compassion, and strength."[13]

Those who follow Jesus are enabled to confront the harsh realities of daily life — to mourn — not because they trust in the power and resources of the world, but because they have confidence in God's fulfillment of God's promises: "they will be comforted." This confidence is based on the fact that God is now at work in Jesus Christ bringing God's promises to fruition. Not only can they anticipate God's final comforting when the kingdom of heaven is fully established, but as they participate even now in the life and witness of the disciple community they are "happy mourners." Only those who see the light can recognize and lament the darkness. Yet the reality of the light gives hope, as well as courage and comfort. Having heard and embraced the offer of the new life of God's reign in Jesus Christ, like the finder of the buried treasure selling all he has "in his joy," they perform the "mourning" gesture of fasting in joy (cf. Matt. 9:14-17).

13. Davenport, *Into the Darkness,* p. 55.

In a culture that take its leave with the blessing, "Have a nice day," embracing the distress of mourning is not encouraged. Indeed, we in North America expend much money and energy trying to keep the bad things of the world at a distance. The hours spent in front of the television set, attending sporting events, or shopping at the mall, are all ways of distancing ourselves, of walling away the injustice and suffering of the world. But of course, despite all of the escapist activities, suffering happens. The church mourning takes the opposite course, as in worship and prayer and presence it is not afraid to walk into the deepest sorrow. When in hope it can do this, indeed when, over and over, it enacts the grief of Gethsemane and the agony of the cross and does not turn away, it is participating in the mourning that Jesus blessed. It is shedding tears that are founded in the certainty that underneath them is holy laughter.

"The choice is not between happiness and grief, but between feeling and numbness. Those who mourn are to be congratulated because they are able to feel. They are willing to live through the depths so they can also experience the heights."[14]

Blessed Are the Merciful

Those who mourn and those who are merciful share a hope that leads to openness and involvement. Mourners are sensitive to the pain and turmoil of the old age in the sure hope that the new age of fulfillment is coming. Those who are merciful are open to the struggle and despair of others. Both reflect the willingness to get involved, to reject a detached, stoic attitude which accepts and learns to live with the injustice, oppression, and suffering of daily life.

> To show mercy is to reach out, even when the other has turned away. It is to entrust our heart, even when the other is untrustworthy; it is to give, even when our gift may not be received. To show mercy is to build bridges across the troubled waters of our shared and fearful lives. Showing mercy is making room for one

---

14. Lois Barrett, *Praying the Beatitudes of Jesus* (Winnipeg, Man.: Resources Commission of the Conference of Mennonites in Canada, 1998), p. 11.

another in our hearts. It is the deepest meaning of hospitality, making a home for the other within our lives.[15]

The merciful are those who forego judgment and offer forgiveness and pardon — even to those who are in the wrong. They go beyond emotion to determined action of unity and solidarity with, and responsibility for, not only the innocent but the guilty as well. Such action conflicts with the expectations of punishment and revenge found within human systems of justice. For example, "In some ancient schools of philosophy, mercy was viewed not merely as dangerous — a danger to rational, sound judgment — but even as immoral."[16] The extravagance of God's mercy surpasses and calls into question every human standard of fairness.

Perhaps the best commentary on this beatitude is the parable of the Unforgiving Servant (Matt. 18:21-35), which Jesus tells in response to Peter's question about how many times he must forgive his brother or sister. Although enjoying the undeserved mercy of his king, the servant denies mercy to the one in his debt. The servant is held responsible: "Should you not have had mercy on your fellow slave, as I had mercy on you?" (v. 33). As expressed in this parable, it is the prior experience of the unqualified forgiveness of God as experienced in Jesus' healing and forgiving mercy that enables the disciple community to be merciful. "The merciful are those who reflect God's acceptance of the unworthy, the guilty, and the ones in the wrong, because the merciful themselves, conscious of their own unworthiness, guilt, and wrong, have experienced God's forgiving and restoring acceptance through the message of Jesus Christ."[17]

A people of hope, those who mourn and are merciful, are a people of courage. Rather than trying to escape the ills of the world, they embrace and care for those the world seeks to discard. Many mainline churches are — or need to be — challenged by these words in new ways. At a time when many of them worry about how to maintain their expensive church facilities for dwindling congregations or make major investments in new facilities, others, hearing a new call in these words

15. Davenport, *Into the Darkness,* p. 58.
16. Davenport, *Into the Darkness,* p. 84.
17. Guelich, *The Sermon on the Mount,* p. 105.

of Jesus, seek to serve in nontraditional ways out of often uncomfortably anachronistic buildings. They are learning from the small storefront mission churches. Living where poverty, alcoholism, and drug abuse, as well as human beings' abuse of each other in a myriad of ways, is pervasive, these churches offer support and hospitality. When sinners — the unworthy, the guilty, the wrong — do not seek out the ministry of the church, the church must go to them. It is all too easy to forget that Jesus brought the gospel of the kingdom not to those who were well off but to those in need, declaring, "I have come to call not the righteous but sinners" (Matt. 9:13).

Much more than occasional programs of outreach or donating money to relief agencies, the church is called to get personally and closely involved. Followers of Jesus can do this because they are the ones who themselves have received mercy. To share the blessings of God's kingdom means to welcome the stranger, to clothe the naked, to feed the hungry, to care for the sick, and to visit those in prison (cf. Matt. 25:34-46).

A People of Divinely Modeled Relationships: The Hungry and the Pure

Does the following line of reasoning sound familiar? As responsible adults, those who participate in the life and ministry of the church should develop a morality for themselves, a code or pattern or way of life that is right and good. Such a morality will be manageable, it will be able to be taught to children, and others within the faith community, and perhaps even the wider society, can be expected to follow a similar code.

While church people might be very comfortable with that approach to morality, Matthew offers a very different perspective: "Be perfect, therefore, as your heavenly Father is perfect" (Matt. 5:48). To hear that as the assertion of a moral code or standard is to miss both the meaning of the word "perfect" and the accent of the verse on the way in which "your heavenly Father" is perfect. "Perfect" is used in the sense of being complete, entire, whole. "Be whole and complete in all relationships," Jesus is saying, "just like God is!" That's why the call to "be perfect" comes as a summary at the end of Jesus' challenging portrait of a righteousness greater than that of the Pharisees of his day (see Matt. 5:20). In Matthew 5:21-47, Jesus sets forth in more detail the moral expectations of those who would follow him in six statements that turn his hearers' understanding on its ear, with this repeated refrain:

"You have heard it said . . . but I say to you. . . ."

Following that pattern, Jesus provides six graphic examples of the radical nature of righteousness within the reign of God. It is not just murder that is the problem, but also the habitual anger that destroys relationships in community and the name-calling that diminishes another person (vv. 21-26). It is not just adultery that is the problem, but any willful lusting that turns another human being into a sexual object (vv. 27-30). It is not just satisfying the legal responsibilities of divorce that is at issue, but also the fact that divorce itself ruptures a God-established relationship (vv. 31-32). It is not enough to hedge one's commitment to tell the truth by a complex network of oaths; embracing honest speech is the necessary ingredient for trustworthy relationships (vv. 33-37). It is not enough to limit retaliation by matching the punishment to the crime; returning good for evil is required of relationships inside and outside the faith community (vv. 38-42). It is not enough simply to love your neighbor — those of your own ethnic and religious group; God's love invites the disciple community to love even its enemies by undertaking positive action towards them (vv. 43-47).[18]

Jesus is not creating a new law here. Rather, he confirms the validity of Israel's covenant law, while at the same time deepening and sharpening its intent, which is to guide people toward the pattern of God's own relationships, leading them to live together in peace and harmony with one another and with God. Jesus' interpretation of the law provides models of a new way of life that have the power to bring the righteousness of the kingdom of heaven into full force. By stripping away all human ploys to avoid the radical implications of obedience to God's will, Jesus reveals the effects of our actions on the concrete situations of everyday life. He calls into question any behavior that harms relationships within community, and, in each case, he offers a new way.

18. James L. Bailey, "Sermon on the Mount: Model for Community," *Currents in Theology and Mission* 20 (April 1993): 90-91.

Blessed Are Those Who Hunger and Thirst for Righteousness

The human experience of hunger and thirst reminds us that we are not self-sufficient; our very survival depends upon resources from outside ourselves. Too often we do not recognize the true nature of our hunger and reach for substitutes: success, security, wealth, or power. The Gospel of Matthew declares that true satisfaction comes not to those who seek the material comforts of food, drink, or clothing, but to those who "strive first for the kingdom of God and his righteousness" (Matt. 6:33). Interpreted within the context of the advent of the reign of God, righteousness means not moral superiority or arrogance but the divinely modeled pattern of relationships. In God's gracious gift of Jesus Christ, an alienated and sinful humanity is offered the reconciling gift of a new relationship with God. By experiencing God's "righteousness" — God's unconditional love, mercy, and forgiveness — those who follow Jesus are transformed into a new people. Through dying and rising with Christ, a new creation comes into existence: a reconciled and reconciling community witnessing to the reality and power of God's love for the world.

As those who are "right with God," the disciple community manifests the fruit of that relationship: the disciples do God's will as interpreted by Jesus' words and deeds. The church proclaims the gospel of Jesus Christ by offering a faithful performance of the gospel. Life within God's new social order issues in behavior which is in agreement with God's will — the rightness of life before God. The criteria for such behavior is not the performance of miracles or the dutiful adherence to rules, but the love of God and of neighbor, as asserted in the "Love Commandment" (Matt. 22:34-40). Thus the church does not only care about how it thinks or believes, but also how it lives, day to day. "Righteousness is *faith* in *action,* the *practice* of *devotion* — it is *doing* the *will* of God."[19] Practicing a way of life goes to the roots of our lives as human beings; the disciple community seeks to practice a way of life that is grounded in God as source, motivation, and authority. It finds its righteousness — the righteousness that satisfies — only in receiving, celebrating, and manifesting the love, mercy, and forgiveness of God.

19. David J. Bosch, *Transforming Mission: Paradigm Shifts in Theology of Mission* (Maryknoll, N.Y.: Orbis Books, 1991), p. 72.

Blessed Are the Pure in Heart

Those who hunger and thirst for God — for God's righteousness — have a clear focus and direction, seeking and trusting only in God. They are called "pure in heart" because their intentions are singular. As Kierkegaard put it, they "will one thing."

Jesus' pronouncement of blessing on the pure in heart reminds us of the first commandment: "You shall have no other gods before me." It also undercuts all idolatries — all that human beings would put in place of and serve other than the God of Jesus Christ. When the Bible speaks of the heart, it refers to the direction of human desires, motives, will, and intentions. "Whatever one's heart is set upon as the goal to which every act is directed is one's god. . . . Only the heart that is single-mindedly set on God, in contrast to idols, can truly be called pure."[20] Trying to balance conflicting loyalties and competing gods, the impure heart is divided against itself. Just as Jesus resisted the temptation to put other "goals" ahead of God's will (Matt. 4:9), so the pure in heart express total devotion, giving their allegiance and loyalty — their faith — only to God. Among such a people the cry, "Create in me a clean heart, O God, and put a new and right spirit within me" (Ps. 51:10), has been answered.

Becoming a people of whole relationships — hungering for righteousness and maintaining singular loyalty to God — requires the mutual support and encouragement of everyone within the church. The good news of God's love and forgiveness does not spring naturally from the human heart or intellect. It can only be communicated from beyond the individual, through the witness in word and deed of faithful followers of Jesus Christ. Christians are bearers and proclaimers of the gospel for and to one another. In order for this to happen, people must be involved with one another, spending time together, getting to know each another, sharing the joys and the sorrows of life. A people hungry for life with God, a people seeking to trust only in God, will engage in practices that shape them into closer conformity to the community for which they hunger and thirst. As they listen for God's word in Scripture, as they offer themselves in prayer, as they discern God's call for their life and ministry, they will begin to share their hopes and

20. Davenport, *Into the Darkness*, p. 92.

fears, their strengths and their temptations. Developing mutual accountability for their personal and corporate discipleship, they will watch over one another in love. In such communities, they will find the motivation and the courage to do God's will, to be performers of the gospel.

A People of Peace:
The Peacemakers and the Persecuted

Immediately following the Beatitudes, the Gospel of Matthew offers two images that emphasize the worldwide and world-affirming mission of the disciple community: "You are the salt of the earth . . ." (5:13) and "You are the light of the world . . ." (5:14). These words are not given as commands or as requests, but as declarations. Those who follow Jesus, those who embrace the new life of God's kingdom, *are* the salt of the earth, they *are* the light of the world. In Jesus Christ, their identity and their vocation have been given to them. The church has a purpose: salt is to do its salting and light is to do its illumining. Acting for the sake of God's right relationships generates a witness that points beyond the church: "Let your light shine before others, so that they may see your good works and give glory to your Father in heaven" (Matt. 5:16).

To live as salt and light, and thus to perform the gospel, is the missional quality of the disciple community — that for which it is sent! Its reason for being is to communicate and to demonstrate the good news of God's new order: "to proclaim Jesus' ultimate victory over the power of evil, to witness to his abiding presence, and to lead the world toward the recognition of the love of God."[21] To make this point, it may be helpful to read the Gospel from the ending backward — to begin with the "Great Commission" (Matt. 28:16-20). Matthew's view of the church does not include withdrawal from the world into a comfortable and self-satisfied enclave. Instead, Matthew envisions a dynamic and intentional community of active and disciplined mission. The community of Jesus' disciples is to be about the business of making disciples, calling others to "turn around" and "then come, follow me." They are to invite others into the transforming relationship with Jesus

21. Bosch, *Transforming Mission*, p. 83.

Christ that they've experienced within the disciple community. Christian discipleship is not simply a matter of individual salvation, but of participation in Jesus' mission to "make disciples of all nations" (Matt. 28:19).

Blessed Are the Peacemakers

Those who would be Jesus' disciples are called not simply to be peace*lovers*, but to be peace*makers*. Anyone can love or desire peace, but the active and intentional making of peace is another matter. The Bible most often speaks of peace as a gift or activity of God. It is God who promises to overcome the alienation and distortion of human life, to bring compassion and justice, harmony and wholeness, right relationships all around — *shalom*. In the healing ministry of Jesus Christ — the "Prince of Peace" — God's reign of love and mercy breaks into the present experience of indifference and cruelty. As the disciple community shares in Jesus' life and ministry, it is called to participate in God's "peaceable kingdom," to live even now as a people of peace. As it performs the gospel, the church becomes an instrument of God's reconciliation — peacemakers. Living as a social reality in the midst of the world, the church is to make God's peace visible through the quality of its life and practice — to be an example and an invitation. "Without such a community, the world literally has no way of knowing that all God's creation is meant to live in peace."[22]

In chapter 18, Matthew demonstrates the active and concrete nature of peacemaking by providing pragmatic instruction in the practice of "loving frankness,"[23] mutual admonition, and forgiveness within the disciple community. Rather than advocating the "adult" virtues of maturity, independence, willpower, and responsibility, Jesus tells the disciples to "become like children" (18:3). To be children is to be dependent, to be vulnerable, to need help, and to be receptive to it. Disciples are those who follow Jesus and seek the kingdom, not those who have achieved perfection and become sinless. They need continually to

22. Stanley Hauerwas, "Living the Proclaimed Reign of God," *Interpretation* (April 1993): 158.
23. John Howard Yoder, "Binding and Loosing," in *Royal Priesthood*, p. 347.

"learn" to be sinners: to openly and truthfully acknowledge their failure to do the will of God and their inability to love one another as God loves them. Only then will they also "learn" to be forgiven: to admit their need for forgiveness, seek and accept correction, and be reconciled with God and one another. The way of discipleship is not the way of the lone ranger. It requires the shared admonition, forgiveness, and guidance of an involved, caring, and supportive community of "forgiven sinners." Just as Jesus suffered for and bore the sins of the world, so Christians — realistically and honestly — are to bear one another's sins. "Forgiveness is the Christlike suffering which it is the Christian's duty to bear."[24] As disciples receive, participate in, and continue the peacemaking manifested by Jesus, "they will be called children of God" (Matt. 5:9).

Blessed Are the Persecuted

As the disciple community committed to the way of life within God's kingdom, the church will threaten and challenge the values and ways of the world. The old order does not eagerly welcome or embrace the new order. The strong winds, heavy rains, and damaging hail of the storm created by God's reign, the storm that disrupts the reign of sin and corruption, was expressed most profoundly in the crucifixion of Jesus. That storm continues today. To be poor in spirit and meek in a world which celebrates strength, to mourn and be merciful in the midst of cruelty, to be pure of heart and seek righteousness in the midst of greed and self-interest, and to cultivate peace where violence rules inevitably results in hostility from those who are dominated by a way of life which relies upon human might and achievement rather than upon God's undeserved love and grace. Recognizing the resistance they would encounter, Jesus warned his disciples: "See, I am sending you out like sheep into the midst of wolves; so be wise as serpents and innocent as doves" (Matt. 10:16).

> What unites those addressed in the Beatitudes and pronounced blessed, is this, that they are driven to the very end of the world

---

24. Dietrich Bonhoeffer, *The Cost of Discipleship* (New York: Macmillan, 1959), p. 100.

and its possibilities: the poor, who do not fit into the structure of the world and therefore are rejected by the world; the mourner, for whom the world holds no consolation; the humble, who no longer extract recognition from the world; the hungry and thirsty, who cannot live without the righteousness that God alone can promise and provide in this world. But also the merciful, who without asking about rights, open their hearts to an other; the peacemakers, who overcome might and power by reconciliation; the righteous, who are not equal to the evil ways of the world; and finally the persecuted, who with scorn and pains of death, are cast bodily out of the world.[25]

Conclusion

The Beatitudes declare that those who look toward God, who cast themselves upon God, who in their attitudes and lives are beggars before God, who are rejected by the world, these are the ones God blesses, "for theirs is the kingdom of heaven" (Matt. 5:10). The gospel of the reign of God, as proclaimed by Matthew in the Beatitudes, shakes and upsets our expectations and standards: the last become first and the first last.

The ethical demands of the Sermon on the Mount are neither utopian ideals nor a new law by which individuals are to live in order to be declared righteous before God. These demands, rather, express the realizable potential of restored relationships among a community of people endeavoring to live within the realm of God's righteousness. The conduct Jesus calls for assumes, creates, and grows out of relationships of wholeness between brothers (Matt. 5:21-26), brothers and sisters (5:27-30), husbands and wives (5:31-32), friends and enemies (5:38-47). This redemptive way of life — life within the reign of God — emerges as members of the disciple community surrender their whole lives to become dedicated (cleansed, set aside) to God. As performers of the gospel, those who live by faith (a people of trust and hope) and who recognize and embrace the way of the kingdom (a people of right relationships and of peace) discover that a transformed relationship with God and

25. Gunther Bornkamm, *Jesus of Nazareth* (New York: Harper & Row, 1956), p. 76.

each other is possible. For them, doing God's will is not a project clothed in fear, obligation, or self-interest. Instead, it expresses the joy, freedom, and mutuality of life within God's kingdom — already begun in their midst. To such as these is promised the joy and the fulfillment of seeing God.

> Who shall ascend the hill of the Lord?
>   And who shall stand in his holy place?
> Those who have clean hands and pure hearts,
>   who do not lift up their souls to what is false,
>   and do not swear deceitfully.
> They will receive blessing from the Lord,
>   and vindication from the God of their salvation.
> Such is the company of those who seek him,
>   who seek the face of the God of Jacob.
>
> (Ps. 24:3-6)